Enjy

Allen Johns

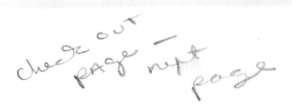

check out
page — next page

Walking

Hadrian's

Wall

Adventures

With

Grandchildren

OTHER BOOKS BY ALLEN JOHNSON

Drive Through Russia? Impossible – 1986

Canoeing the Wabash
Adventures with Grandchildren – 1991

Biking Across the Devil's Backbone
Adventures with Grandchildren – 1997

Australia from the Back of a Camel
Adventures with Grandchildren – 1999

Biking to the Arctic Circle
Adventures with Grandchildren – 2000

Genealogy of the Johnson Family – 2001

Rollerblading Across Holland
Adventures with Grandchildren – 2002

Kayaking Around Iceland
Adventures with Grandchildren – 2003

Willmore Horseback Adventure
Adventures with Grandchildren – 2004

Sweden Through the Eyes of a Six-Year-Old
Adventures with Grandchildren – 2005

Walking Hadrian's Wall

Adventures With Grandchildren

Allen L. Johnson

Creative Enterprises

Dayton, Ohio

PHOTO CREDIT

Page 3 . . . . **English Heritage**
Page 14 . . . . **D.J. Woolliscroft**
Page 16 . . . . **Navigator PR**
Page 65 . . . . **Crown MNR**
Page 72 . . . . **National Museum of Scotland**
Page 88 . . . . **Alan Sorrell**
Page 89 . . . . **Vindolanda Trust**
Page 90 . . . . **Robin Birley**
Page 92 . . . . **Philip Corke**
Page 94 . . . . **Jarrold**
Page 96 . . . . **R.J.S. Bertram**
Page 105 . . . . **AirFotos**
Page 106 . . . . **English Heritage**
Page 141 . . . . **Gordon Young**
Page 175 . . . . **David Robinson**
All other photos . . . . **Author**

FIRST EDITION

Published by Creative Enterprises
1040 Harvard Blvd; Dayton OH 45406-5047

Printed by Sheridan Books Inc
Ann Arbor, Michigan

Manufactured in the United States of America
ISBN: 1-880675-09-9

DEDICATION

This book is dedicated to my wife Gloria, who is currently undergoing treatment for mesothelioma canser. She has supported me on these adventures with our grandchildren for the past 15 years and participated in many of them. I also wants to thank the following people for their editorial and proofreading assistance:

Karla Brun
Linda Chigi
Margaret Cotton
Hannah Grove
Connie Johnson
Gloria Johnson – chief editor and consultant
Linda Schwartz
E.J. Stannard

CONTENTS

ILLUSTRATIONS

TITLE   **PAGE**

TITLE	PAGE

x

Walking

Hadrian's

Wall

Adventures

With

Grandchildren

Chapter 1

Do We Have to Walk the Whole Way in One Day?

"How would you like to search for Roman coins, visit King Arthur's Camelot and hike a 2,000-year-old wall from sea to sea?" I asked our 11-year-old twin granddaughters, Emily and Jessica during the winter of 2004/2005.

"Do we have to walk the whole way in one day?" Jessica asked.

"No, dear. We'll walk about 10 miles a day for 10 days. You can stop and rest whenever you want."

"Is that the same King Arthur we read about that had a round table and did good deeds?" Emily asked.

"Yes it is. They're not exactly sure of the location of his castle, but we'll visit one of the places they believe it might have been."

"Do we have to carry our bags with us as we walk?" Emily asked.

"No, we'll have your Aunt Connie and Cousin Linda come along and drive a van to carry our luggage," I said. That's how our plan to go to England and walk Hadrian's Wall from the North Sea to the Irish Sea started.

In AD 120, the Roman empire, Hadrian, decided to build a wall across England to protect the Roman settlements in the south from the Barbarians in the north. He chose to start the wall near Newcastle and end at the Solway Firth since that was the narrowest part of central England. The Wall stretches 80 miles across the rugged English countryside. A force of 100,000 Roman soldiers and engineers quarried one million limestone blocks to face the ten-foot-thick, fifteen-

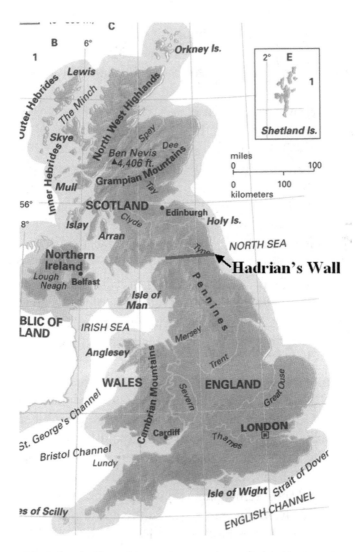

Hadrian's Wall is located near the Scotish Border

An artist's rendition of the original Wall

foot-high wall. Imagine the Herculean effort it took to chisel block after block from the local quarry, transport the heavy blocks to the site, hoist them up onto the wall and cement them in place. The center of the wall was filled with rubble. Every mile, the soldiers constructed a milecastle to house thirty soldiers and every third of a mile they built a watchtower to house ten soldiers. The entire Wall was completed in about three years, a monumental achievement. Supporting forts were built a few miles behind the Wall at fifteen-mile intervals to house 500 cavalry to support that section of the Wall. The result is the most remarkable monument to four centuries of Roman rule in Britain.

During the spring of 2005 I discussed the walk plans with my wife, Gloria, and granddaughters to flush out our itinerary. We planned to hike about 10 miles a day, stopping often to visit ruins of milecastles, museums, local historical sites and picturesque English pubs. Much of the Wall has been dismantled over the past 2,000 years and the stone used to build churches, barns, farmhouses and city buildings. Many of the buildings we planned to visit display plaques and art work purloined from the ancient wall. During the excavation of one fort, a hoard of over 13,000 Roman coins dated before AD 350 was discovered in a well. The brass, silver and gold coins are now on display at the Black Gate Museum in Newcastle. We would follow the Hadrian Wall Path National Trail, which was just opened in 2003. Prior to 2003 there were private sections of the Wall path that were not accessible to the public. Through the work of the British National Trust and the United Nations Educational, Scientific and Cultural Organization (UNESCO), the Wall has been designated a World Heritage Site and the entire length is open to the public.

Emily and Jessica had read about King Arthur and the round table and were excited about seeing that part of history. We planned to take them through the Roman fort Camboglanna, near Carlisle, which is believed to be King Arthur's Camelot. King Arthur and his knights fought many battles along Hadrian's Wall and he died in battle there. According to local history he was buried at Avalon, the Roman Fort Avalanna.

It will also be fun to expose the granddaughters to the difference between American English and British or Anglo-Saxon English. They'll learn:
a burn is a small stream,
a crag is a steep, rugged rock cliff,
a fells is a hillside,
a firth is the waterway where the tide meets the river current,
a gorse is juniper,
a lough is Celtic for lake (loch),

a moor is a boggy area of wasteland ,

a tarn is a small, steep-banked mountain lake,

a vicus is a small group of people who provide day labor to support the Roman legions and

a wolds is an elevated track of uncultivated land.

To prepare for the 100-mile walk Gloria, Emily, Jessica and I started taking long hikes around Dayton, Ohio in the spring. We started out with a 5-mile hike and then added an extra mile on each subsequent hike. I made certain the route took us by a Dairy Queen so we could stop for refreshments on the way. On the first 5-mile hike we took our 12-year-old Labrador retriever, Sarabi. At about the 4-mile point, Sarabi lay down in the grass to take a nap. Jessica finally coaxed her into getting up and completing the hike. Sarabi was the only one who had trouble completing the 5-mile hike.

Our daughter-in-law, Connie, would be our van driver. She had driven the van 2,000 miles supporting my bicycle ride to Alaska in 1999, but always drove on the right side of the road. Connie expressed some concern about driving on the left, British style. "It's not hard," I assured her.

My cousin, Linda, planned to walk part of the Wall with us and navigate for Connie when necessary. A month before departure (Friday the 13th), Linda fell down the stairs at home and broke her ankle. "I'd still like to go," Linda said. "It'll probably be the only chance I'll have to see the Wall." By the time our departure date rolled around, Linda had graduated from a wheelchair and crutches to a cane and a soft cast on her ankle. "I'm going!" she announced.

After months of intense preparation, Gloria, Emily, Jessica and I packed our bags (Appendix A) and drove to the Cincinnati Airport to catch our Delta Airline flight to London.

Chapter 2

The Backstreet Boys Are On Channel 15

"Do they use dollars over there?" Jessica asked as we drove to the Cincinnati Airport.

"No, dear," I said. "Their currency is the British pound and pence. They used to have shillings and crowns as coins, but now they've gone to 100 pence to a pound just like we have 100 cents to a dollar."

After I parked the car in the long-term lot, we checked in at the Delta Airlines counter and took the tram to the gate.

"There's Aunt Connie!" Emily yelled as Connie pushed Linda's wheelchair toward the gate. They had arrived at different gates, Connie coming from St. Louis and Linda from Chicago, but had met on the way to the London departure gate.

"How was your flight?" I asked Linda as we all hugged each other.

"It was good," Linda said. "They had a wheelchair to take me from the counter to the gate in Chicago and then they had a wheelchair for me here."

"How does your ankle feel?" Gloria asked.

"It itches like mad," Linda said. "I got out of the hard cast last week and have a walking cast that I can take off at night. I've graduated from the crutches to a cane so I'm a little more mobile."

Our Boeing 767 Delta flight took off at 6 PM and headed over Canada, Greenland and Iceland toward London. I sat with Emily in the center block of seats while Jessica and Gloria sat across the aisle from us by the window. Emily and

Jessica immediately started exploring all 20 channels of the plane's audio system and sharing their discoveries with each other.

"Listen to channel 7," Emily told Jessica as she discovered a catchy country-western tune on her headset.

"Channel 15," Jessica said a few minutes later as she found The Backstreet Boys' latest release. Emily and Jessica switched channels every few minutes until supper time.

After a tasty steak meal we all watched a movie and got a few snatches of sleep before the flight attendants woke us for breakfast.

The pilot set the big jet down very smoothly on the London Gatwick runway in a misty drizzle. The Delta staff met Linda at the plane's door with a wheelchair and pointed the way to immigration and customs.

"Will they search us?" Emily asked as the immigration agent stamped our passports.

"I don't think so," I said as we searched for our luggage. It took three luggage carts to hold all our bags.

"I hope you are getting a BIG car," Linda said as she surveyed the mound of bags on the carts.

We passed through the green "Nothing to declare" line and into the Gatwick arrival lounge without anyone asking to search our luggage. I went immediately to the Barclay Bank ATM machine to get some British pounds.

"WE CANNOT COMPLETE THIS TRANSACTION" the Automatic Teller Machine (ATM) screen informed me when I requested £200. I then went to the Currency Exchange window and gave the cashier a $100 bill. I got £53 and a few pence in exchange. The exchange rate had fallen dramatically since I visited Britain a few years ago.

As we left the arrival lounge and walked toward the Hertz Rental building Gloria, Emily and I pushed the luggage carts while Connie pushed Linda's wheelchair. The carts had four-wheel steering and Gloria's cart started going sideways as she passed a driveway sloping toward the street.

"I can't control this dumb thing!" Gloria yelled as the cart skittered down the ramp into the street.

"The carts have a mind of their own," Connie said as she ran up, grabbed ahold of the cart and helped Gloria muscle it back up onto the sidewalk.

I signed the Hertz paperwork for a blue Ford Galaxy seven-passenger van and we started loading the luggage. Emily agreed to sit in the back seat and we loaded bags all around her until she was buried and completely out of sight.

"Are you okay back there?" I asked.

"Yeah, I'm okay," Emily replied. "Just throw me some candy or peanuts occasionally so I don't starve."

I slid in the driver's seat on the right side of the van and tried to prepare myself for driving on the wrong side of the road for the next two weeks.

"Be sure to yell if I start to pull onto the right side of the road," I told Gloria who was in the left-hand copilot seat.

"Okay, if I'm awake," Gloria said, her eyes already drooping from jet lag and lack of sleep.

I started up the M-23 motorway toward London, turned west onto the M-25 and came to an immediate stop with a massive tailback (traffic jam). The cars inched along at a few miles per hour (mph) for about 30 minutes until we passed the construction area. Then I could speed up to about

60 mph. We circled around the west side of London and turned north on the M-1. Everyone else in the van was sound asleep by the time we reached our turn at Leicester. I had reserved rooms at a Holiday Inn in Leicester for our arrival day, but I wasn't sure exactly where it was. I expected to see a Holiday Inn sign along the motorway. Dream on! No signs, so I stopped at a BP petrol station and asked directions.

"Go right at the first circle and then straight into the center of town," the attendant told me. A half-hour later we found the downtown Holiday Inn.

"You don't have reservations here," the clerk informed me. "Can I see your confirmation?" I pulled out my confirmation e-mail and showed it to the clerk.

"Oh, you have reservations at our Holiday Express."

"And how do I get there?"

"Easy. Go east on St. Agnus. Turn left on Nottingham and then a right on Secome. Take a right on Walnut and a left on Beford. Follow that until you see Franklin. The Holiday Express will be on your right," the clerk told me.

Navigating the narrow streets of Leicester proved to be a real challenge. The street signs are on the side of the corner buildings and sometimes they are painted over or missing. We eventually found Walnut after driving around in circles for 10 minutes, but couldn't find Beford.

"It must be that street with no name," Connie suggested as we exhausted all the other possibilities.

Beford was a narrow two-way street with cars parked on both sides reducing it to one car width. Halfway down the block I met a car coming the other way. I had no choice but to back up. Very slowly I backed all the way down the street and let the car pass. Then I drove back up Beford praying I wouldn't meet any more cars.

"There's the Holiday Express sign!" Linda shouted as we reached Franklin Street.

It took another few minutes to follow the sign to the hotel. The Holiday Express turned out to be an ultra modern hotel with bright, clean rooms. Everyone else collapsed in their rooms after we carried the luggage in. I headed out to find an ATM and locate a restaurant for supper.

"The Local Heroes is a nice family pub," the hotel clerk suggested. "It's about three blocks up that way," he said, pointing north.

I found a National Westminster Bank ATM, got £200 and headed up to find the Local Heroes. It was located in a small shopping mall. I checked the menu and it appeared general enough to satisfy everybody in our party. Then I went back to the hotel and worked on my journal. My philosophy dealing with jet lag is to stay up until bedtime on the arrival day, walk around, get plenty of sunlight and try to reset my body clock.

About 5 PM the others woke up from their nap and complained about being hungry. We all walked up to Local Heroes and found a big booth to hold the six of us. We ordered a combination of cottage pie, baked salmon and fish and chips, sampling each other's order to get an idea of what British pub fare tasted like. It was great!

After supper we walked back to the hotel. Emily and Jessica turned on British TV in their room and complained that they couldn't find any cartoons. I was more interested in the bed. It was still light when I dropped off to sleep.

Chapter 3

Can We Play in the Ocean?

"Haven't these people ever heard of Cocoa Pebbles?" Jessica asked, surveying the breakfast bar in the hotel. "The only cereals they have are corn flakes and something that looks like cat food."

"That's granola and it is very good for you," I said as I dished up a bowl of granola for myself. "They have juice, fruit, cheese and croissant rolls too."

After breakfast, we packed up and were on our way north by 9 o'clock. We stopped for gas and lunch at a service area on the M-18 motorway. It had a McDonald's restaurant so the grandchildren could order some familiar fast food.

As we approached Newcastle there were a lot of turn-off options, but none of them mentioned our destination, Whitley Bay, so I continued straight into downtown Newcastle. Bad idea! We encountered heavy traffic, narrow streets and a minimum of signs. I knew our accommodations were on the North Sea so I turned right and we wound our way toward the water. A half-hour later we reached the sea. I made a lucky guess, turned left and found the Marlborough Hotel, an old three-story Edwardian house.

"Can we play in the ocean?" Emily asked as we pulled into the hotel parking area.

"Not right now, dear, but we will this evening," I told her.

The hotel door was locked and had a "back at 3:00" sign in the window so I suggested we drive to Wallsend where

11

we would be starting our walk the next day and visit the museum.

In AD 120, the Romans built the Segedunum (meaning strong fort) on the Tyne River to form the east end of Hadrian's Wall. The 300-foot square fort housed a mixed cavalry/infantry force of about 500 men. The walls and buildings were made of quarried limestone. The fort was active for about 300 years and then fell into disuse when the Roman Empire started to disintegrate in the fifth century. As villages started to spring up in the area during the following centuries, builders found that "borrowing" stones from the fort and wall was easier than quarrying new stones so the fort slowly disappeared stone by stone. By the 18th century, the area was a grassy meadow. In 1777 high-quality coal was discovered under the fort and several shafts sunk to mine it. For the next hundred years coal mining was the dominant activity at the fort site. By the end of the 19th century, the coal was depleted and a shipbuilding company took over the site. The shipyard occupied the north bank of the Tyne River down the hill from the fort site and low-cost housing was constructed on the fort site for the shipyard personnel. In the early 1970s, the run-down terrace housing at the fort site was cleared in preparation for construction of new housing. Renewed interest and funding for Hadrian's Wall preservation allowed the Department of Archaeology at Newcastle University to purchase the site and start excavation of the fort. Over the next 25 years, funding was obtained to completely excavate the site, reconstruct part of the wall and bath house and build a modern museum including an interpretive center to relate the 1,900-year-old story of the Roman fort. Today the Segedunum can lay claim to being one of the most extensively excavated forts in the

We saw the foundation of the real Wall and a replica

Roman Empire and certainly to being one of the most comprehensively understood on Hadrian's Wall.

"Are those real gold coins?" Emily asked as we viewed the museum exhibits.

"Yes they are and that's just a small part of the coins they recovered," I said. "They found 13,000 Roman coins in a well at one of the forts."

"Did the men wear dresses?" Jessica asked, pointing to a soldier wearing a tunic.

"They didn't have pants like we have," I explained. "The rich Romans wrapped a piece of cloth around them called a tunic. The ordinary people wore a sack-like dress. The soldiers did wear a pair of tights under their blouse so they could ride on horses."

We walked out of the museum and across the street to examine the remnants of Hadrian's Wall. There we discovered

13

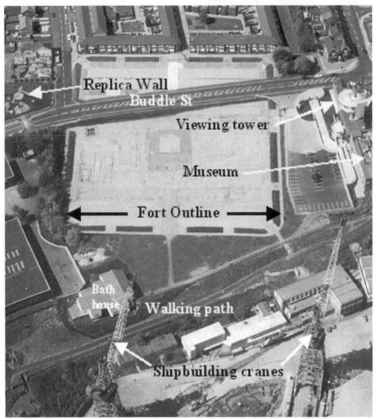

Aerial View of Segedunum at Wallsend

the foundation of the original Wall and a replica section of the Wall.

"These stones look really old," Emily said looking at the discolored foundation stones.

"They are," a man working nearby said. "Almost 2,000 years old." The man was the museum guide for this exhibit.

"What happened to the rest of the stones in the Wall?" Jessica asked.

"People borrowed them to build their house or their church," the guide said.

"That's vandalism to tear someone's wall down," Emily said. "Why don't they make them bring them back"

"After the Romans left, the stones didn't really belong to anyone so people just borrowed them," the guide said. "It wouldn't be practical to make people tear down their homes or churches to rebuild the Wall."

"Can we climb up on the Wall?" Jessica asked.

"Sure, that's what it's for," the guide replied.

Emily and Jessica scampered up the steep stone stairs to the top of the Wall. Gloria and I climbed up at a more leisurely pace. We could see the outline of the entire fort from the top of the Wall, an impressive sight. Present-day Buddle Street cuts the fort in half. After getting a feel for the Wall, we went back in the museum and up to the viewing tower which rises 100 feet above the fort. From there we could see the Tyne River, the shipbuilding facility, the fort and the park where the replica Wall section is located.

"The fort was as big as a small city," Jessica said.

"That's right," I said. "Over 500 people lived in the fort and they had all the things you would have in a small city: barracks to house the men, stables for the horses, a granary to store their food, a water storage tank, blacksmith shops, armory for their weapons, dining halls, a hospital, baths, big meeting halls and shrines to their gods."

"Are we going to follow Hadrian's Wall through the city streets?" Emily asked.

"No, dear. None of the Wall is visible in the city. We'll follow that asphalt walking path down the hill from the fort,"

15

Hadrian's Wall Path Passport

NATIONAL TRAIL

I said pointing to an abandoned railroad bed that had been turned into a walking/bicycling path.

After reading the posters describing what we were seeing from the viewing tower, we took the elevator back down to the museum.

"Where do we get the Hadrian's Wall Path Passport?" I asked the museum cashier.

"I can give them to you and stamp them," she said. "How many do you need?"

"There are six of us."

"Do you plan to do the entire walk?" she asked.

"Yes we do."

"You should plan on at least seven days for the walk," she suggested.

"We plan to take ten days," I said.

"That's even better," she agreed as she stamped six passports and handed them to me. "Leave them open for a few minutes so the ink will dry without smudging."

The Marlborough Hotel was open when we arrived back in Whitley Bay. I walked in and met Allen Thompson, who with his wife, Hilary, own the hotel. We had talked on the phone and noted that we both spelled out first name the same way.

"Hi Allen, I'm Allen," I said as we shook hands.

"Glad to meet you Allen. You have rooms 5, 8 and 22. Room 22 is on the ground floor and the other two are upstairs."

"Great. My cousin has a broken ankle and can't climb stairs so she'll be in the ground floor room."

We unpacked the car and took our bags up to our rooms. Then Emily, Jessica and I took a quick trip down to the beach to check the water temperature.

"It's cold," Jessica said as she stuck her hand in the North Sea.

"That's why they call it the North Sea," I said.

The girls picked up a few pretty stones and then we walked back to the hotel.

"I'm hungry," Gloria declared.

"Me too," everyone else chimed in.

We all ordered spaghetti at Mama Rosa's. Emily and Jessica asked for lemonade to drink.

"This isn't lemonade," Emily said as she took a sip of the clear, bubbly drink. "It's Sprite!"

"They call 7-Up or Sprite lemonade here," I said.

We topped off the meal with "Death by Chocolate" cake—delicious!

After supper I took everyone else back to the hotel and then Connie and I went out for a driving lesson. Fortunately, the van had an automatic transmission so Connie didn't have to worry about shifting gears left-handed.

"Just remember you are supposed to be by the center line of the road," I said as she started down the road at 10 mph. "Turn right here."

Connie reached for the turn signal lever and turned on the windshield wipers.

"The turn signals are on the opposite side to American cars," I said.

"Yes, I noticed," she said as she hit the correct lever for the turn signal. We went around the block a couple of times and then back to the hotel. Connie did fine on her first encounter with a right-hand drive van.

"Do you think you'll be okay tomorrow?" I asked.

"Yes, as long as there isn't too much traffic," Connie said

Gloria and I went to bed early. Emily and Jessica went to Connie's and Linda's room and had a tea party until all hours.

Chapter 4

Are We Lost Already?

"They have enough food to feed an Army," Jessica said as the owner's wife took our orders for breakfast: Cereal, yogurt, stewed prunes, grapefruit, bacon, sausage, eggs, pancakes, toast, marmalade, orange juice, coffee, tea and milk, but no Cocoa Pebbles.

"We have a long walk today so eat a good breakfast," I told Emily and Jessica. They did.

I drove through Newcastle to South Benwell to show Connie and Linda where to wait for us at the end of our day's walk.

"I'd suggest you park in this industrial parking lot and wait for us," I said.

"Is there a restroom close by?" Connie asked, looking up and down the row of industrial buildings.

"I don't see a gas station or convenience store, but you could probably go into that office right there and use their toilet," I suggested, pointing to the nearest building.

As I headed back through downtown Newcastle, I got lost. They didn't think about parallel and perpendicular streets back in the Middle Ages when they settled Newcastle. People followed the cow paths or rivers and that's the way the streets developed. I headed east and eventually found a street that was on my map. It took me a half-hour to find the Segedunum, our starting point. Connie and Linda had all day to find their way back to South Benwell.

"Have a good walk," Connie said as we packed our maps, water bottles and snacks in our backpacks.

After petting the five stray cats and getting lost we finally started our walk

"Call us on the radio," Linda suggested. I had brought a pair of two-way walkie-talkies to keep in contact with the van. We tried the radios and they came in loud and clear.

"Bye Aunt Connie," Emily said as Connie and Linda drove out of the parking lot.

"Which way do we go?" Jessica asked.

"Down the hill," I said as Gloria, Emily, Jessica and I started on the Hadrian's Wall walk.

Emily and Jessica ran ahead, skipping down the cobblestone street. Gloria and I followed behind. We passed under a stone viaduct and came to the parking lot of a shipbuilding company.

21

We saw a lot of wildflowers along the walking path

"There's a cat," Emily said, pointing to a calico cat sitting on the warm hood of a car in the parking lot.

"There's two more under the car," Jessica said, squatting down to pet them.

"And another one by those food dishes," Emily said pointing to cat dishes by the front door of the shipbuilding office.

"I don't see any way out of here," Gloria said, looking around the parking lot.

"Are we lost already, Grandpa?" Jessica asked.

"Yes," I admitted. We hadn't even started the walk and we were already lost. That could be a bad omen. I walked in the shipbuilding office and asked the receptionist where Hadrian's Wall walk started.

"After you pass through the viaduct, there is a set of steps on the right that will take you up to the walkway," the lady said.

"Thank you," I said as I walked back into the parking lot.

"Did you find out where we start?" Emily asked.

"Yes, right up there," I said pointing to the top of the viaduct.

"You mean we have to climb straight up the wall?" Emily asked.

"No, there are stairs on the other side of the viaduct."

We walked back under the viaduct, up the stairs and started down the eight-foot wide asphalt walkway toward Newcastle.

"Was the Wall along here?" Jessica asked as we passed the shipyard with its huge shipbuilding cranes.

"No, the Wall ran along the top of the hill, but now it's under the streets and buildings of the town. A railroad track ran along this path. After the railroad stopped operating, the city made the railroad bed into a walking or biking path. I don't think we'll see any more of the Wall until tomorrow."

"Why don't you try the radio and see if you can contact Connie?" Gloria suggested.

"Connie, this is Allen. Can you read me?" I called on the two-way radio I brought to keep in touch with the van.

No answer. I tried several times with the same result. The radios only work line-of-sight. If there are buildings or a hill in the way, they don't work. We were down the hill from where we started, which probably explained why we couldn't contact Connie.

"Look at all the wildflowers," Gloria said as we followed Emily and Jessica along the path. There were pink wild roses, yellow daisies, purple foxgloves, white Queen Anne's lace, yellow elephant ears, a perfectly rounded puffball dandelion-like flower, blue cornflowers and purple clover.

We only met a few other walkers and their dogs along the trail. A Swiss gentleman we talked to said he expected it would take him seven days to walk the Wall.

"Do you plan to walk to the other end, young lady?" he asked Emily.

"Yes. I came to England to walk the Wall and I'm going to walk the whole thing," Emily said.

"I don't know if I'll walk all that way or not," Jessica admitted. "It depends on how I feel."

As we walked on Emily found an earthworm trying to crawl across the path. She picked it up and moved it over to the other side so it wouldn't get stepped on. Jessica found a snail shell at the edge of the path.

"Can I take it home?" Jessica asked.

"I think there is still a snail inside," I said. We peered into the shell and saw two antennas and a little face staring back at us. "You'd better put it back in the grass or his mother will wonder what happened to him." Jessica put it back where she found it.

We came to a switchback where the path doubled back on itself and ran down the steep hill to the Tyne River. Gloria and I followed the gradual-sloping path down while Emily and Jessica ran straight down the steep hill through the field of white and yellow daisies to the river. A tugboat chugged up the river as Emily and Jessica waited at the bottom of the

Emily and Jessica cut down the hill rather than following the switch-back

Gloria and I followed the path and caught up with the twins beside the Tyne River

hill for us to catch up. They waved to the tugboat pilot. He waved back and gave them a toot on his air horn.

As we approached downtown Newcastle, the riverside changed from rural to urban. Beautiful brick apartments lined the bank with magnificent gardens displaying gigantic yellow roses, red torch ginger and other exotic flowers. The first bridge we came to was the Millennium Bridge. It is a walking/cycling bridge shaped in a horizontal arch and supported by cables running up to a similar vertical arch. When a ship comes up the river, the horizontal span is drawn up to the vertical span by the cables, which resembled an eye winking.

We stopped to rest under a 15-foot diameter golden grid globe in the heart of the business district. Dozens of

Purple foxglove flowers we encountered by the river

Red and yellow torch ginger growing by the path

The Millennum Bridge in downtown Newcastle

office workers sat by the river eating their lunch. Several "executive lunch wagons" lined the street next to the river. I walked up to the lunch wagons and bought sandwiches, soft drinks and some dessert cakes. We joined the other river-watchers and enjoyed our executive lunch.

"Have you caught any fish?" Emily asked a fisherman holding a 10-foot-long pole with a gigantic saltwater reel.

"Yes, I've caught a few perch today," the Britisher said. "Yesterday I caught a four and a half pound codfish. I also get salmon, flounder and whitefish out of the river."

We continued on, passing under four more bridges before we came to the western edge of downtown Newcastle. The sun came out and the temperature rose into the high 70s.

We ate lunch under the globe in the business district

"How much farther?" Gloria asked as we reached the 10-mile point in our walk. "I'm getting hot and tired."

"We still have a couple of miles to go," I said. "You can wait here by the river while I go get the car and then I'll come pick you up."

Emily agreed to wait with Gloria in a little shaded park while Jessica and I hurried on to find Connie and Linda. About 30 minutes later we crested a hill and could see the industrial area where the van should be. I turned on my radio and called Connie.

"Where are you guys?" Connie answered on the radio.

"We're at the top of the hill, about three blocks from you. See you in about 5 minutes."

Jessica and I hurried down the hill. Connie gave each of us a hug as we got to the van.

"How was the walk?" Linda asked Jessica.

"It was pretty long," Jessica said. "And Grandpa wouldn't let us play in the river."

"You got to play by the river when we stopped to rest and when we ate lunch," I said in my defense.

"Yeah, but only from the sidewalk," Jessica said. "You wouldn't let us climb over the railing and go down to the river bank."

"You're right. It was too muddy."

"Did you have any trouble finding your way here from Wallsend?" I asked Connie as I drove back to pick up Gloria and Emily.

"Just a little," Connie said with a laugh. "Before we left the parking lot, we asked a lady about the way here. She gave us a pretty simple route, a lot shorter than the way you drove."

"We only ran three red lights and went down a one-way street the wrong way," Linda added.

"We kept calling you on the radio every 20 minutes while we waited for you," Connie said. "The people coming by looked at us kind of funny so we made up a cover story in case they asked us what we were doing."

"We planned to tell them that President Bush was coming to Newcastle next week and we were Secret Service agents with the advanced party checking out the security along his parade route," Linda said.

"A florist came by with a big bouquet of flowers and asked us for directions to some address," Connie said. "We

We stayed in the Marlbrough Hotel in Whitley Bay

told him we were tourists and weren't even sure where we were."

We picked up Gloria and Emily and drove back to our hotel in Whitley Bay. Emily, Jessica and I walked down to the North Sea while Gloria, Connie and Linda went to their rooms to rest. The water was perfectly clear, but cold. Emily and Jessica waded knee-deep in the sea, looking for shells and pretty rocks.

For supper we drove to the center of Whitley Bay and ate at the "Ritzzy Restaurant." A Pakistani man and his family ran the restaurant. He told us he had worked in restaurants in New York City before coming to England. We had delicious lentil soup and a T-bone steak that I could cut with my fork.

Emily wading in the North Sea

Jessica ordered vanilla ice cream for dessert. Emily only likes chocolate ice cream and they didn't have any.

"Shall I bring anyone else a spoon so you can sample the girl's ice cream?" the owner asked.

"Yes," Linda and Connie agreed.

"Small spoons!" Jessica suggested.

The owner came back with a big dish of vanilla ice cream and two gigantic industrial cooking ladles. The spoons had 18-inch-long handles and a 4-inch-diameter bowls. The whole dish of ice cream would have fit in one of the spoons.

"Ahhhh," Jessica yelled, as she put her hands over the ice cream to protect it.

Jessica looking for shells and rocks in the North Sea

"Can you show the girls how to fold the napkins?" Connie asked, pointing to the fan-shaped napkins the owner's son had put on our table.

The son came back to the table and spent about 10 minutes teaching Emily and Jessica how to fold the napkins into the fan shape.

Gloria and I went right to bed when we got home from supper, but Emily and Jessica went down to Connie's and Linda's room for a tea party before going to bed. Kids don't ever get tired.

Chapter 5

Gloria! --- Gloria!

A field full of big blue lupines and bright orange flowers covered the hillside and gave off a sweet aroma as we climbed up the hill from the industrial area into the rural countryside. The smooth paved path gave way to a dirt trail following the route of the Wall. Emily and Jessica skipped on ahead picking wildflowers and chasing butterflies. Gloria and I plodded along behind, huffing and puffing after the steep climb.

We walked past an abandoned Vickers-Armstrong industrial complex that used to produce and fabricate steel. One small corner of the huge building housed a coal yard--the rest of the steel-frame building stood rusting and empty.

We followed a nice paved path early in the day

The paved path gave way to a muddy trail

Dozens of pigeons and blackbirds flew in and out of the broken windows.

The wide grassy path leveled off at the top of the hill and wound through the trees. Gloria and I walked along enjoying the pleasant breeze and the moderate 75°F temperature. What a perfect day for walking the Wall.

"What is that big tepee?" Jessica asked, pointing to a giant brick cone rising 100 feet in the air.

"The guidebook says it is the remains of the Lemington Glass Works," I said thumbing through my Hadrian's Wall Path guidebook. "They used to make glass in that cone."

"Can we pet the dog?" Emily asked as a gentleman approached us with a small salt and pepper colored Yorkshire terrier.

Emily and Jessica stopped to pet the Yorkshire terrier

"Ask the man," I suggested.

"Can we pet your dog?" Jessica asked.

"Why, yes," the gentleman who appeared to be in his late 70s replied. "Sasha would like that."

"How old is she?" Emily asked while she rubbed the dog's belly.

"Sasha is 10 years old. I used to have a black chow named Rex when my children were young. It was very protective of my children. I could leave the dog guarding the baby in the pram on the sidewalk while I went in the butcher shop to get a roast and Rex wouldn't let anyone get near the pram. Now that my wife is dead and my children grown and gone, I got a little lap dog. Are you walking the entire Wall?"

"Yes," Emily replied. "We just started."

"My wife and I walked it years ago. There were some wild areas along the Wall back then. One area in the Northumberland National Park is very hilly and still heavily forested. Not long ago they discovered the remains of a Spitfire World War II fighter and a Lancaster bomber. Do you plan to visit any of the castles in the area?"

"Yes, we are planning to see Warwick Castle on our day off," I said.

"There are two other castles you ought to see while you are here: Bamburgh Castle about 10 miles south of Holy Island and Alnwick Castle another 20 miles south of that. Both are very historic and in good repair. The Armstrongs still live in Bamburgh Castle."

The gentleman was very friendly and decided to walk a ways with us.

"I grew up in this area and used to work in the nearby coal mines," he said as we walked briskly down the path. "They are all closed down now. I still live in a cottage over the hill near where I grew up."

"GLORIA!" a ghostly voice called. *"GLORIA!"*

"Yes, Lord," Gloria answered, looking up through the tree-covered canopy.

"DOWN HERE!" the voice commanded. *"DOWN ON THE ROAD!"*

Our path had merged with a country lane and Linda and Connie sat in our van at the side of the lane. "We're lost!" Linda said. "How do we get to Newburn?"

"How did you find us?" Gloria asked.

"We've been driving around in circles trying to find the bridge and we saw you on the path," Linda said with a laugh.

The chances are a million to one that we would be walking along the one spot where the road and path merged just when Linda and Connie drove by. It is hard to believe our meeting was purely by accident. I tend to believe in divine intervention.

"You just follow this road straight ahead about three miles," our English companion said.

"We'll meet you for lunch by the bridge on the south side of the village," I suggested.

"We drove through that village several times and couldn't find the bridge," Linda said.

"When you get to the edge of the village, the road forks," the gentleman advised them. "Take the left-hand fork and you'll find the bridge."

"Okay," Linda said. "We always went straight at the fork. See you in a little while."

"I have to leave you now," our companion said. "It has been nice talking to you."

"It was a pleasure," I said. "Thanks for the information on the history and the castles." The people we've met along the wall have all been very friendly and helpful.

Thirty minutes later Emily, Jessica, Gloria and I walked into Newburn and found Linda and Connie at the Boathouse Inn by the bridge. The menu at the Inn featured a variety of mouth-watering lunches.

"The chef is off at a wedding today so we're not serving lunch," the barmaid said.

"Do you have anything we could eat?" I asked.

"I could heat up some meat pies," she suggested.

"Fine. Six meat pies, please," I said. The pies were tasty and we followed them with chocolates for dessert.

"What is that marker near the roof on the outside wall of the Inn?" I asked the barmaid as I paid our bill.

"That's the high water mark," she replied.

"You mean the river flooded that high?" I asked.

"It happened back in 1883 when the Krakatoa volcano exploded in Indonesia. The tidal wave rose 30 feet above the normal river level here and we're 25 miles inland from the North Sea. The water came in through the front door and filled the room almost to the ceiling before it receded. When the lads went home soaking wet, their wives thought they had gotten drunk and fallen in the river."

"We'll meet you at Heddon-on-the-Wall in a couple of hours," I told Connie as we left the Inn.

We hiked along the river watching the pleasure boats cruising up and down. At the bend in the river a mother black duck was teaching her baby duckling to fly. The duckling climbed on the mother's back and then the mother would run across the water, flapping her wings rapidly for 100 yards before settling back down in the water. She did that three or four times before she slid her duckling off her back and let him try it for himself. He flapped his wings and ran across the water, but failed to become airborne. After about five tries the mama and baby paddled over to the shore to rest.

"Can we get an ice cream cone?" Jessica asked when we came to a park with an ice cream wagon in the parking lot.

"Good idea," I agreed.

I bought four ice cream cones and then we stood and watched people water skiing on the river. There must have been 100 people in the park skiing, picnicking and walking their dogs. A couple walked by with two large gray terriers with strange haircuts. Most of the fur was cut short, but the fur on their heads was long. The lady said it was called a "Roman Cut."

As we started walking down the grassy path alongside the river we passed a field full of blue forget-me-nots, some purple foxgloves and yellow snapdragons. The snapdragons had at least 100 blossoms on each stem. The bottom 50 buds were in full bloom while the top 50 were still inside their green wrappers.

"Look at the horses!" Emily shouted as two huge Percheron plow horses walked down the path, followed by their handler.

"I'm taking them to the east field," the man said.

"I like your horses," Emily told the plowman as he walked by us.

We passed a dozen wild rhododendron bushes full of huge pink flowers. Their sweet scent had attracted hundreds of wild bees, which swarmed noisily around the blossoms.

"This looks like a golf course," Gloria said as we passed green manicured fields next to the river. Sure enough we came to the greens and saw a few golfers.

The Wall path cut right across the fairway of the fourth hole. Signs warned hikers to beware of flying golf balls. We looked both ways and walked briskly across the fairway when no golfers were in sight. Our walk to that point had been basically flat along the river, but now we started up a 400-foot high hill to the village of Heddon-on-the-Wall. We passed several farms with sheep, cows and horses. The dirt road became muddy as we passed through thick woods. Half way up the hill we stopped to rest by the side of the road.

"How much further?" Gloria asked as we caught our breath.

We found another section of the wall at Heddon-on-the-Wall

"About another half mile," I said.

We climbed up and up and up. As we finally arrived at the village, we saw a bride in her long red dress and groom in black tails coming out of a church and heading for the City Hall where their reception was being held. Connie and Linda were sitting by the Three Tuns Inn.

"They asked us to come to the reception," Linda said. "We went in the Inn to use their rest room and the whole wedding party was in there before the wedding. They invited us to the wedding and reception."

"Where's the Wall?" Gloria asked.

"It's supposed to be on the east side of the village," I said as we piled in the van and I drove around looking for it.

42

"There it is!" Emily shouted as we passed a substantial section of the Wall. I parked the van and we walked over to it. This was the first we had seen of the Wall since we started at Wallsend. The 100-foot long section was about 4-feet high. I took photos of our group by the Wall to document our walk.

From Heddon we drove to Durham, about 15 miles south of Newcastle, to visit the castle there. We arrived just as the castle tours ended so we parked in the center of town and walked through the market. Emily and Jessica bought some candy and some souvenir bears. Then we stopped at a restaurant and had fish and chips for supper.

When we got back to our hotel, Emily, Jessica and I walked down to the beach while the others went to their rooms to rest. Emily and Jessica took off their shoes and waded in the North Sea looking for shells and rocks. I found a pink egg-shaped rock while Jessica found the perfect skipping rock--three-inches in diameter and one-fourth inch thick. We counted 22 skips the first time she threw it. She retrieved her skipping rock and threw it a dozen more times. Emily found a flat rock, but never got more then 10 skips with hers.

While we were skipping our rocks, a group of about a dozen young men came down to the beach 100 yards from us. The men, in their early 20s, stripped naked and ran screaming into the North Sea. I kept watching Emily and Jessica, who were busy skipping their rocks, and the girls never once looked down toward the naked boys. Later that night, the girls had a tea party with Connie and Linda and told them in vivid details about the nasty boys.

Chapter 6

Our Street is Flooded

"Ouch!" Jessica yelled as she scraped her leg on the sharp stone wall. We started our walk from Heddon-on-the-Wall and Emily and Jessica were walking on the ledge of the stone wall adjacent to the road. Jessica had tried to climb past some bushes growing near the wall and cut her leg in the process. I got my first-aid kit out of my backpack, cleaned the cut with an alcohol pad and applied Neosporin and a Band Aid.

Hadrian's Wall actually ran UNDER the road we followed. Back in the 1700s, the British built a military road on top of the remains of the Wall. The Heritage Walk follows the road for several miles. The defensive ditch was still visible on one side of the road and the vallum on the other side. The thick clumps of thistles and thorns that grew alongside the road reached out and grabbed at Emily and Jessica's bare legs. We had been advised to bring warm clothes, waterproof jackets, wool hats and gloves because the weather in northern England was usually cold and rainy in early June. This day had dawned warm (75°F) and sunny so Emily and Jessica opted to wear shorts and a T-shirt for their hike. After an hour of getting their legs scratched by the thorns they agreed that jeans would have been more appropriate for the walk. I used almost an entire tube of Neosporin doctoring the scratches on the twins' legs.

The path switched from the roadside of the stone fences to the field side a little outside of Heddon. Every field contained

It was warm enough for Emily and Jessica to wear shorts

sheep and every ewe had a lamb. The ewes shepherded their lambs away from us as we passed through each field.

"Why do they have so many gates or stiles?" Jessica asked.

"I know," Emily said eagerly. "To let the people through but not the sheep. The sheep don't know how to climb the steps or unlock the gate."

Many of the fields had groups of square stones lying about, remnants of the Wall. Some of the field walls were also made from the Wall's stones.

"Here is a cocoon," Jessica said pointing to a large, gray cocoon attached to a small tree branch. "I wonder where the butterfly is?"

"There's a white one," Emily said, pointing to a butterfly flitting around a yellow flower. "I wonder if it came from that cocoon? Can we take a break?"

"Sure," I agreed. We sat down in the shade of a beech tree to eat an apple, have a drink of water and rest. Jessica sat with her back against the tree, while Emily stood leaning against the other side. As we got ready to leave, Emily backed around the tree and fell over Jessica's outstretched legs. Emily tumbled over backwards dramatically, feet flying in the air and arms spinning in circles.

"Are you hurt?" I asked.

"No," Emily and Jessica answered simultaneously.

A little further along we met a man and woman coming along the path the other way.

"We haven't seen any kids walking the Wall," Emily said. "Have any children walked the entire Wall?"

"I'm sure some kids have completed the walk, but probably not many," I said. "One hundred miles is a long way for kids to walk."

Emily and Jessica started singing the DARE song they learned at school to pass the time.

"Do we dare, do we dare? Yes we do, yes we do." After going through that song a couple of times they switched to "Jesus Loves Me." The time goes faster when you're singing.

The previous day when we stopped at the Durham Market, Emily bought a variety bag of candy that had dozens of different kinds in it. Jessica opted to spend her money on a beanie baby. As we hiked the Wall, Emily would occasionally dig into her candy bag for a snack. She always offered Jessica some of her candy. One of the candies was shaped like a cheeseburger. Emily dissected the candy, giving the cheese and pickle to Jessica and keeping the meat and bun for herself.

"What does it taste like?" I asked the girls.

"The bun is peach flavored and the meat tastes like cherry," Emily said.

"The cheese taste like bananas and the pickle like a lime," Jessica said.

"Pretty complicated for a nickel's worth of candy," I said.

As we passed along a field full of wild poppies, Emily and Jessica each picked a small bouquet. Then the path took us between two hedgerows where the bushes and small trees grew over the top making a shady tunnel. The path climbed steadily upwards to the top of a big hill and then started down the other side to a large reservoir below. Emily and Jessica started skipping down the hill and skipped all the way to the bottom, leaving me a quarter mile behind. They sat down on top of the stone wall surrounding the reservoir and waited for me to catch up.

As we continued along the path, the walking surface changed from grass to dirt to mud to gravel to crushed limestone to two-foot square flagstones to wooden planks and back to grass. The twins were in good spirits: laughing, joking, singing, giggling and talking as we walked. A little after noon we came to Robin Hood's Inn where we were to meet Gloria, Linda and Connie for lunch. As we walked up to the front door, I noticed an alcove where they kept the Hadrian's Wall stamp. I took out our passports and stamped them to show we had completed this section of the walk. Then we went in.

"We're over here," Connie yelled from the far corner of the room.

47

"They said they were booked up when we got here," Linda said, "but they eventually found us a table for six. Apparently everyone goes out to eat for Sunday dinner and this is one of the few restaurants in the area."

Almost every table had a complete range of ages, from babies to adults and seniors—three generations. The Sunday menu consisted of leg of lamb, pork roast, roast chicken, prime rib of beef with Yorkshire pudding and trout. We took the time for a proper Sunday dinner with all the trimmings. Jessica ordered vanilla ice cream for dessert and they even had chocolate ice cream—Emily's favorite. Gloria and I opted for fresh strawberries in sweet cream—mouthwatering!

It was a psychological challenge to pry myself up from a big, delicious Sunday dinner and head out for a six-mile hike along the Wall, but I did it. As Emily, Jessica and I arrived at the first farm field we spied a big red-tailed hawk sitting in the middle of our trail eating something, probably a field mouse. When we got within about 100 yards of it, the hawk took off and flew to the center of the field to complete its meal. The bird took off without a sound and flew silently, like an owl.

We continued along the path without seeing any signs of the Wall since it was under the road in this area. We occasionally saw the defensive ditch, the vallum or stones indicating we were still on the right path. The Heritage Walk is well marked with yellow acorn markers and arrows so it would be hard to get lost.

As we passed near a farm house we encountered beautiful red and yellow torch ginger flowers, each blossom seven- or eight-inches high. On the other side of the farm, the path went through a field full of brown Jersey cows. A thousand-pound cow lay right along the path. Emily walked

Emily had a nice conversation with the cow

cautiously up to it, talking in a soothing voice all the time. The cow looked at Emily, mooed and continued to chew her cud as Emily walked on past her.

A few miles beyond Robin Hood's Inn, we came to a Roman quarry where the soldiers obtained the limestone for the Wall. The Romans dug quarries every five miles or so along the wall since it was hard to transport the heavy stones very far.

"Can we run down to the bottom of the hill?" Emily asked as we rested by the quarry.

"Yes, you can."

The twins ran down and back up the quarry hill at least three times before stopping to rest with me. Walking 12 miles isn't enough exercise for 11-year-old girls. They have to run up and down hills, climb trees and make a few side trips to use up all their youthful energy.

From the top of the quarry hill we could see our van parked alongside the road at our pickup point. After the girls finished playing in the quarry we headed for the van. Emily and Jessica ran the last 100 yards to the van. Kids never seem to tire out!

"We have time to drive to a Roman Fort before we go back to the hotel," I told Gloria, Connie and Linda.

"Okay," they agreed.

We drove to Corbridge, a Roman fort predating the Wall. It was built in about AD 60 and housed about 500 infantry and cavalry soldiers. Most of the fort has been excavated and it provided a good example of how a typical Roman fort was constructed. The attendant gave us each audio gadgets that told the story of the fort. By pressing the number on the audio machine corresponding to the number of the building we stood by, the machine would relate the purpose and history of that particular building.

The granary had a raised floor to allow air to circulate under the grain to keep it from spoiling. Emily and Jessica climbed under the granary floor to investigate the building's construction.

"It's hard to believe this building is 2,000 years old," Jessica said as she reemerged at the far end of the building.

"I didn't think anything that old would be still standing," Emily admitted.

We saw the strong-room in the basement of the headquarters building where they kept the money to pay the soldiers, in addition to the barracks, the bath, the hospital and the stables.

After touring the excavated site we went into the museum. It contained a rich collection of artifacts found at the site: body armor, weapons, jewelry, decorative jugs and coins. One of the drawings showed what the Fountain House probably looked like.

"That building was beautiful," Jessica said. "It had statues and big columns and a fountain. I didn't know they built such modern-looking buildings that long ago. I expected it to be made of wood and mud."

"The fountain had a practical purpose also," I said, reading from the drawing. "Water which has flowed for quite some time in a closed pipe needs to be allowed to mix with air to restore its freshness before drinking. That was the purpose of the fountain and aeration tank."

"Look at those dark clouds with the golden sun peaking through," Connie said as we drove home. "It looks like we're going to get some rain."

And rain it did. The rain came down in buckets, so hard the windshield wipers couldn't keep the windshield clean. I slowed down and tried to stay between the white lines on the road.

"Can we stop for ice cream?" Emily asked.

"Okay," I agreed. "What do you want to do about supper?"

"I'm still full from lunch," Gloria said. "Why don't you buy some snacks and we'll skip supper."

Everyone agreed so I pulled into a BP petrol station that had a convenience store. The place was mobbed. On Sunday all the regular stores are closed so the petrol station convenience stores are the only show in town. I picked up a variety of snacks, some ice cream bars and soft drinks and

An hour after the rain stopped, the runoff continued to pour down the retaining wall

waited in line for about 15 minutes to check out. The cloud burst continued while I was in the store and I had to wade through four inches of water to get back to the car.

As I drove into Whitley Bay, the traffic was backed up for blocks. I finally realized that the streets along the beach were closed, including the one our hotel was on. I drove up and down side streets until I got close to the hotel and parked on a side street that only had a few inches of water in it.

"We'll have to wade home," I advised our group. Everyone took off their shoes and we waded to the hotel. It looked like a circus. Hundreds of people stood down by the beach-front streets watching the spectacle. The water in front of our hotel was a foot deep. A fountain three-foot high spewed out to the sewers as the pressure of the runoff from up the hill

Emily and Jessica splashed in the rainwater rivulet

pushed the rainwater to the ocean. The steps down to the beach were foot-deep waterfalls. The golden sun was shining on the North Sea and the rain clouds had moved off to the west.

"Can we play in the water?" Emily asked.

"I think it would be okay now," I said. "Let's go up and get our swimming suits on."

We waded to the front door of our hotel and met Allen T, the hotel owner.

"I've been here 15 years and I've never seen it rain as hard as it did today," Allen said. "I hope our basement didn't flood."

After getting our swimming suits on, Emily, Jessica and I climbed carefully down the steps to the beach holding

After the rainwater stopped flowing, Emily and Jessica played in the North Sea

onto the railing for dear life. The water was still three-or four-inches deep cascading down the stairs. The runoff had cut ruts in the beach several feet deep as it poured over the rim of the street down onto the beach. An hour after the rain stopped, there was still enough water pouring off the street to create several rivulets 25-foot wide and two-foot deep. The water rushed down the beach so fast it created two-foot high standing waves. Emily and Jessica played in the rivulets, running back and forth through them, breaking down the sand banks at the edge of the rivulets and splashing in the warm rain water. As the rivulets grew shallower, Emily and Jessica ventured out into the North Sea deeper and deeper until they were up to their hips. They played in the North Sea until the

sun started to set. No nasty boys to ruin their beach time this
night.

Chapter 7

This Branch Makes a Perfect Bed

"I don't feel well," Connie said as we stopped at the Shell station in Heddon-on-the-Wall to pick up some snacks. "I ache all over and feel nauseous." Her hands were shaking and she looked pale. "I don't think I'll be able to drive the van today."

We had checked out of the Marlborough Hotel in Whitley Bay and planned to move to the Centre of Britain Hotel in Haltwhistle. Not having a van driver threw a new wrinkle in the works. It was obvious that Connie needed some medical attention so I drove to Haltwhistle and stopped at the Chemist (pharmacy) there. Connie described her symptoms to the chemist, which in Britain is also the first-line medical aid in the small towns.

"It sounds like you have the flu," the chemist said. "I can give you some pain pills and medicine for the nausea. If you're not feeling better in a day or two, I'd suggest you go to surgery and see the doctor."

After we got the medicine, we then drove to the Centre of Britain Hotel and arrived there about 9:30 AM.

"Good morning," I said to the hotel clerk. "We have reservations for three rooms for tonight, Johnson, party of six. My daughter is ill and I wonder if one room might be available now so she could rest?"

"I'll check," the lady said. She rang the housekeeper and discussed the situation.

"Yes, we have one room you could use now."

I signed the register and the lady gave me the key.

56

"It's the first unit on the left out that door," she said, pointing to the back door.

I drove the van back to the unit and unloaded all of our luggage. Connie went in and laid down in the bed while we moved the luggage into her room.

"You and Linda stay with Connie," I suggested to Gloria. "I'll drive the van to the Wall and find someone to give us a ride to where we'll start our walk today."

"Okay," Gloria agreed.

Emily, Jessica and I drove to Chollerford where we planned to finish our walk. I parked at a petrol station and we all went in.

"Good morning," I said to the attendant. "My grandchildren and I are planning to walk Hadrian's Wall today and we need a ride down to Halton. Do you know anyone who might give us a ride this morning?"

"We have a taxi in town that you could take," the attendant said. "Would you like me to call him?"

"Yes, please."

The attendant rang the taxi and he arrived five minutes later.

"Where to?" the young taxi driver asked.

"About 10 miles down the road to Halton," I said. "We plan to walk the Wall back to here."

"Are your children going to walk too?" the young man asked.

"Yes, they plan to walk the whole Wall."

"You have a perfect day to do it," he said. "This is the finest week of weather we've had this year."

The taxi driver let us out where we finished our walk the day before. I paid the £7.30 fare and gave him a £2 tip. "We may need to call you again tomorrow," I said.

As we walked across the entrance to a farm field, Emily stepped between the iron bars on a cattle grate and skinned her shin. More Neosporin and another Band-Aid. Talk about the walking wounded!

"Do you think you'll be able to walk on it?" I asked before we started off.

"Yes, I think so," Emily replied.

"Let me know if it starts to hurt," I said.

We started out and were soon walking along the deep, v-shaped vallum. Thick clumps of gorse grew along the sides of the vallum and clusters of small blue flowers.

"Can we stop for lunch?" Emily asked about a half-hour into the walk.

"Good idea," I agreed. We set our backpacks down alongside a farm wall and took out our lunch: Pringles, yogurt, apples, cheese and fresh rolls—a delicious picnic.

Jessica leaned back against a sign on the farm wall that cautioned: "Lambing—take special care." About that time a pair of Royal Air Force jet fighters zoomed over our head, not more than 100-foot above the ground.

"**RRRRRRRRRRooooooooaaaaaaaaaammmmmmmmm!!!!!!!**"

The racket made us all duck our heads.

"I guess they didn't see the sign," Jessica said as she looked up. "That noise would scare a poor, little lamb to death."

After we finished our lunch we packed up and continued our walk. In the middle of the field we encountered

We crossed through a dark forest on Stanley Plantation

a flock of sheep, each with a young lamb. We crossed to the other side of the vallum so we wouldn't scare the lambs. At the far side of the field we entered a dark pine forest. The trees grew so close together that no sunlight reached the ground. The path was bare dirt and mud, no grass at all. My topographical map identified the forest as part of Stanley Plantation.

"My tooth is loose," Jessica said as we walked through the forest. "I can wiggle it, see."

"I can pull it for you," I offered.

"No!"

When we got through the forest we sat down on the edge of the vallum to rest.

**The constant westerly wind caused the tree to grow
lopsided**

"You know, I think I was a slave in a previous life,"
Jessica said very seriously.

"You believe in reincarnation?" I asked.

"Oh yes," Jessica said. "Sometimes I dream things
and they seem very real. I'm sure I'm looking into my past
lives. I believe I was a pioneer in one life and an Indian another
time. I'm really interested in nature and I think that comes
from my past lives."

"How about you, Emily? Did you have any past lives?"
I asked.

"I think I lived as a cat in my past life," Emily said
with a smile. "I love cats."

Jessica found a perfectly curved branch to rest on

As we started out, a big European hare darted out of the field and hopped down the lane. We climbed a big hill and as we reached the top, I pointed out a tree that leaned to the east.

"Do you know why all the branches on that tree are on one side?" I asked.

"It's because the wind always blows from that direction," Emily said.

"You're right. The branches find it easier to grow down wind."

"Can I climb this tree?" Jessica asked as we reached a giant beech tree with twisty branches reaching all the way down to the ground.

"Yes," I agreed.

Emily found a nice tree branch to rest on also

Jessica scampered up one of the branches and curled up in the sweeping curve of a big branch.

"This branch makes a perfect bed," she said.

Emily found a suitable branch on the other side of the tree and climbed up. They rested there for about 10 minutes and then climbed down and we continued our walk.

An hour later we came to another 50-foot long section of Hadrian's Wall in a field. This section is interesting since it shows the foundation of the wide wall (10-foot wide) and the narrow wall (7-foot wide). Each section we find seems to be bigger and better than the last. The further inland we go, the better preserved the Wall is. Down the hill from that section is Brunton Turret one of the best-preserved watch towers in the entire wall. This tower has 11 courses of stone standing

We keep finding higher and longer sections of the Wall

about 8-foot high at the tallest part. The size of the watch tower is plainly visible, but its original height is a matter of conjecture. Most historians believe the tower was three stories high with the bottom floor housing the soldiers, the second floor giving access to the top of the wall and the third floor for watching.

"How many soldiers would have stayed here?" Jessica asked.

"They think there were probably eight or ten soldiers at each watch tower," I said.

"That isn't much room for so many people," Emily observed looking around the 10-foot square ground floor.

This is the most complete watch tower we encountered

"Some of them would be sleeping or eating on the ground floor," I said. "Others would be working on the second floor and a couple would be watching on the top floor."

After admiring the tower we continued down the hill and across the Tyne River into Chollerford. The Chollerford Bridge consisted of five beautiful stone arches over the wide North Tyne River. It was built in 1775 after the great flood of 1771 destroyed the old bridge. About 500 yards below the current bridge are the remains of the Roman bridge built 2,000 years ago.

We walked to the petrol station where we left our van to get a snack.

Artist concept of original watch tower on Hadrin's Wall

"I'll have ice cream," both girls said simultaneously. Surprisingly they had both chocolate and vanilla. After we finished our ice cream, I drove back to Haltwhistle.

"How is Connie feeling?" I asked Gloria when we arrived back at the hotel.

"She seems to be feeling better," Gloria replied. "She took a hot bath and went to bed for awhile. I think she is up now."

Connie was feeling well enough to go to supper with us. We ate in one of the hotel dining rooms, a 15-foot by 25-foot low-ceiling room with 5-foot thick stone walls.

"This building was a fortified farm house 1,000 years ago," Grace, the hotel owner's wife told us. "They kept the animals in this downstairs portion and lived in the upstairs. It is the oldest building in the town. We used to have a bed and breakfast in the Bellister Castle down by the river until they built a bypass road right through our property. That Norman

Castle dating from the 14th century, burned down several times. The last time was in 1904 when the insides burned. We had eight bedrooms and an office there. There was a tunnel that led from the castle to this house. The entrance and exit are still accessible, but the middle section of the tunnel collapsed after one of the fires," she told us.

We leisurely ate our way through a scrumptious three-course dinner over the next two hours. We had a fresh garden salad with deviled eggs, olives and mushrooms for a starter. That was followed by French onion soup with croutons and topped off with prime rib au jus, grilled trout almondine or leg of lamb with mint sauce. The children opted for a dessert of ice cream (Emily got chocolate for the fourth time in two days) while the adults chose cherry crumb cake with sweet cream and hot tea. Afterwards, Gloria and I went out to walk off our supper. Then I read a little more about the history of the area. The book about the Roman fort at Housesteads mentioned a bastle house, a fortified stone house common in this area:

"The Border trade (cattle thieving) was so great a mischief that all the considerable farmhouses were built of stone in the manner of a square tower, with overhanging battlements, and underneath the cattle were lodged every night. In the upper room, the family lodged, and, when the alarm came, they went up to the top and with hot water and stones from the battlements, fought in defense of their cattle." We had eaten supper on the first floor of such a bastle house.

Chapter 8

How Old is Your Daughter?

"Can I have pancakes this morning?" Emily asked the waitress at the hotel dining room. "I'm tired of cereal."

"I'll see if the cook can make them," the waitress said.

The Centre of Britain offered a full cooked English breakfast of eggs, bacon, sausage, potatoes, fried tomatoes and kippers, but Emily didn't want any of that, just pancakes. The cook agreed to humor her. Emily devoured three pancakes smothered in maple syrup.

Our rooms were not in the 1,000-year-old section of the hotel, but new bungalows in the back courtyard. Our three identical bungalows included a 10-foot by 15-foot living room

The Centre of Britain Hotel in Haltwhistle

We stayed in new bungalows in the hotel courtyard

with couch, desk, closet, built-in dresser drawers and TV. The large bath/shower/sauna was in back of the living room. A narrow staircase led up to an open A-frame loft area with a double bed. A wooden railing kept clumsy people from falling out of the open loft. The woodwork was a blonde knotty pine. The rooms were efficient and comfortable.

Connie still didn't feel up to driving so Emily, Jessica and I drove the van to the petrol station at Chollerford. Before we started our walk, we decided to tour the Roman fort there. It started raining lightly when we walked from the petrol station to the fort ruins. As we entered the fort grounds, a colorful cock pheasant darted across the grassy path and stopped on the far side to scratch for something to eat.

"What a pretty bird," Jessica said. "What kind is it?"

We encountered a pheasant at the Chesters Fort

"It's a pheasant just like the ones we have back home. They are very good eating."

"You better not!" Emily said. "It's too pretty."

"The Romans brought them to Britain as a food source. People still hunt them for sport and food here and back in the U.S.," I said.

We walked down the wet grassy path to the ruins of the bathhouse by the Tyne River.

"Look at all the snails," Emily said, pointing to the grass around the bathhouse. There were hundreds of one-inch long black snails or slugs crawling across the path and wiggling through the grass. "They must have come out because of the rain," she said.

Emily explored the hot bath at Chesters Fort

Chesters was a cavalry fort with a strength of about 500 men. As usual, the bathhouse was built outside of the fort walls. The Chesters bathhouse has been extensively reconstructed. The twins toured the changing room, the warm bath, the hot room or sauna, the hot bath and the cold bath. The Romans built a furnace near the center of the bath and stone hot air ducts under the floor to warm the various rooms. An aqueduct brought water into the bath from upriver. After it was heated, the hot water ran through tiles to the baths. The bath provided an opportunity for the Romans to relax and socialize with their fellow soldiers. They spent hours in the bath, not just a quick wash up and out.

After touring the bathhouse, we walked down to the river to see the remains of the 2,000-year-old Roman bridge across the Tyne River. The course of the river had changed slightly in the past 2,000 years so the east supports for the bridge stood on dry land, 50 or 75 feet from the river's edge. The supports for the near side stood in the middle of the river, 20 or 30 feet out from the current west bank. It is hard to imagine that any part of the bridge survived for 2,000 years.

After an extensive tour of the bath and bridge we walked up to the museum, which was on the site of the Roman fort. Before we toured the museum, I stamped our Wall passports with the Chesters stamp. A display of the construction of the Wall dispelled the notion that it was built by slave labor. In addition to regular soldiers, the Roman legions contained architectural engineers, surveyors, masons, carpenters and glaziers--all the skills required for the most massive building tasks. Another display showed the plaques taken from the Wall identifying which centurion built each section. A Roman centurion or officer commanded 80 to 100 men and was responsible for building a section of the Wall, usually 100 yards long. A quarrying team would dig the stone, an engineering team would lay the foundation and then the centurion and his men would start building the 10-foot thick wall. The outer faces of the wall consisted of finished limestone block and the middle was filled with rubble, broken limestone and gravel. Upon completion of a section of the wall, the centurion put up a plaque showing he built that section and to what legion he belonged. As Hadrian's Wall disappeared, people took the plaques down and used them for decoration in their homes, stores or churches. The museum had collected dozens of the plaques for display.

"Are these coins real?" Jessica asked as she stood in front of a large display of Roman coins.

We saw Roman coins at the Chesters Fort museum

"Yes, they are real 2,000-year-old Roman coins," I replied.

"Where did they find them?" Emily asked.

"When they excavated these old sites, they find some of the coins around the buildings," I explained. "At one site they found a pottery vase that had 2,000 silver coins in it, all dated between AD 250 and AD 300. At another fort they dug in the well and found 13,000 gold, silver and brass coins from around AD 350. They think the people must have hidden them in the well when the barbarians attacked the fort."

"I'd like to find a Roman coin," Jessica said. "Can we keep any coins we find while walking the Wall?"

"I guess so," I said.

The museum had an extensive collection of sandals, iron tools, jewelry and paintings showing aspects of the Roman occupation. After an hour-long tour of the museum we walked back to the petrol station and had the attendant call the taxi.

The same taxi driver showed up. "I'm the only taxi in the village," he admitted. "Where to today?"

"We'd like to go to Housesteads today," I said. "We plan to walk back here from there."

Emily, Jessica and I piled into the backseat of the taxi and he started up the road. About 15 minutes later he pulled into the Housesteads parking lot. I paid him and we walked to the gift shop to buy some snacks for the hike.

Housesteads is the best-preserved fort along the Wall. It is situated on top of a big hill, 400 feet higher than the parking lot. We climbed for half an hour just to get up to the fort. Sections of Hadrian's Wall run for a mile and a half in both directions there, the most complete part of the entire Wall. This site is the most visited of any along the Wall. Tour operators bring busloads of tourists to Housesteads for day walks. While we saw very few walkers along the previous sections of the Wall, we encountered dozens of walkers as we started hiking from Housesteads. The area is very hilly and we climbed up and down the steep muddy path.

"Can we stop for lunch?" Jessica asked.

"Yes," I agreed. We found a couple of big rocks to sit on and opened our backpack. I had packed sandwiches, Pringles, cheese, an apple, raisins, a chocolate snack cake and a candy bar in a plastic bag for each of us. It was very windy and halfway through lunch, the wind grabbed Jessica's empty plastic bag and carried it 50 feet up in the air. Both Emily and Jessica jumped up and started chasing it. They ran down the

Near Housesteads we enountered a long section of Hadrian's Wall

hill chasing after the bag, but it continued to fly 100 feet or more ahead of them. The faster they ran, the faster the bag flew. Before they ran out of sight, I gave them a loud blast on my whistle (all three of us carried whistles around our necks to signal each other if necessary). I waved my arm for them to come back. Reluctantly, they turned around and climbed back up the hill. I watched the bag fly on and on until it finally snagged on a branch of a hedgerow and stopped. After we finished lunch, the girls walked back down the hill and retrieved the errant lunch bag. Then they cut up on a diagonal to meet me at the Wall on top of the hill.

"This is called Sewingshield Crag and that lake is called Broomlee Lough," I said, pointing over the cliff to the lake a

The Wall follows the crest at Sewingshield

mile away. "Years ago, a wealthy farmer who lived by the lake put all his valuables in an iron chest and hid it in the lake when he learned that robbers were headed his way. They say he never went back for his treasure so it is supposed to still be on the bottom of the lake. The legend says the only way to recover the treasure is to hitch two perfectly matched oxen to a chain made by a seventh-generation smithy, hook it to the chest and drag it up from the bottom of the lake."

"Why can't we just get a scuba tank and dive down to get the treasure?" Emily asked.

"According to the legend you need the perfectly matched oxen and seventh-generation chain," I said.

Broomlee Lough held a sunken treasure

"How would you ever get two perfectly matched oxen?" Jessica asked. "Emily and I are identical twins, but we aren't perfectly matched. I don't think you could do that."

"You're probably right," I said. "That's why no one has ever recovered the treasure."

"How come there are such steep cliffs here and not where we walked yesterday?" Jessica asked.

"These cliffs are called The Whin Sill," I said. "The guidebook describes a sill as a horizontal layer of rock and whin is the common term miners use for the hard, dark colored rocks you see. This sill formed millions of years ago and has tilted over time. Erosion exposed the face of this layer. Because of the tilt of the layer, the north-facing edge is very steep and then it slopes down gradually to the south making a

Emily and Jessica climbed atop the Watch Tower ruins
perfect barrier to protect the Romans from the northern
barbarians."

While the girls rested at the top of the cliff, I climbed
down the 200-foot high face of the cliff to get some photos
looking back up. I climbed back up and we continued on
along the path.

The girls talked about perfectly matched oxen, metal
detectors and chains for the next half-hour as we hiked past
long sections of exposed wall, observation turrets and
milecastles. We stopped and rested on remains of the turrets
and talked about what it must have been like for the Roman
soldiers living there 2,000 years ago.

"They didn't have TV or a CD player or anything to
entertain themselves," Emily said.

I climbed down Sewingshield Crag to take a photo from below

"But they had board games and outdoor games to keep them busy," I said. "They spent most of their time working or keeping warm or drinking."

"I'm sure glad I live in modern times," Jessica added.

"Me, too," Emily seconded the thought.

It started to sprinkle again so we donned our rain jackets and kept hiking. A man and his daughter came up the hill towards us. The girl had long brown hair and was the first child we had met on our walk. She looked about the same age as the twins.

"Good afternoon," I greeted them.

"Hello," the man answered.

"How old is your daughter?" I asked.

"He's my son, and he's 11-years old," the man said.

We explored the Temple of Mithras at Carrawbrough

"Oh, I'm sorry," I said, visibly embarrassed.

"That's okay," the boy said with a laugh, "it happens all the time."

"Grandpa can't tell a boy from a girl," Emily teased me after we were out of earshot from the boy.

"He had a pretty face," I said in my own defense.

We came to the Mithraeum at Carrawbrough.

"This is a Roman Temple," I told the twins. "The Romans worshipped many gods. Mithras was a Persian god that the Roman officers worshipped."

"What's written on these stones?" Jessica asked as she knelt in front of three stone altars.

"Those are altars with inscriptions of praise to their gods."

"I can't read a word of it," Jessica said.

Jessica tried to read the Latin instriptions on the altars

"That's because it's written in Latin, the ancient language of the Romans."

After exploring the temple, we hiked up the hill and came to a jumble of house-sized limestone blocks littering the defensive ditch in front of the Wall. Apparently the Romans didn't think it was worth the effort to move those blocks. Emily and Jessica thought they looked like a challenge so they raced each other to see who could climb to the top of all the blocks first. I rested by the Wall and took photos of the girls.

"Look at that bird standing still in the air," Jessica said, pointing up to a kestrel hovering above the Wall.

"It's called a kestrel," I said. "We have them back home. They can hover in one spot while they are hunting for a field mouse."

The twins climbed on the boulders at Limestone Corner

"That's cool," Emily said. "I've never seen one before."

As we sat down on the Wall to rest, a bunny rabbit hopped out of the tall grass and ran into its hole right under where Emily sat.

"Did you see that?" Emily asked. "I thought he was going to run right into me."

A mile further along the Wall we came to a forest with hundreds of rhododendron trees, not bushes. The trees grew 25-feet high and some places there was a 20-foot high solid wall of pink rhododendron blossoms.

As we approached the end of our strenuous 12-mile hike, Jessica started lagging behind.

"I'm tired," she complained as Emily and I waited for her to catch up.

We found a wall of lavender rhododendrom blossoms

With one mile to go, Jessica picked up the pace.

"I think I can smell the ice cream from the snack bar," she said as she shot ahead of Emily and I. We almost had to run to keep up with her. A few minutes later we jogged into the petrol station. Jessica got a vanilla ice cream bar while Emily and I took chocolate ones to celebrate the successful completion of the first 50 miles of our Hadrian's Wall walk.

We drove back to the hotel. Connie was feeling better. She and Linda had found the Laundromat down the street and done the wash.

"We also found a Goodwill shop and bought a few things," Linda said.

"They had a cat in the shop," Gloria said. "A beautiful calico cat with a bell on its collar."

Jessica ordered gingerbread chicken men for supper

We walked across the street to the Manor House Pub for supper. Jessica ordered gingerbread chicken men with chips (French fries), baked beans and peas. The chicken was cut in the shape of gingerbread men and they didn't get away.

Chapter 9

The Knight Kissed the Loathsome Worm

"You mean we don't have to walk today?" Jessica asked as she dug into her grapefruit at breakfast.

"That's right," I said. "We are taking a well-deserved day of rest. I think we might tour a Roman fort and a modern castle."

After breakfast we drove to nearby Vindolanda, a Roman fort dating from AD 85, 40 years before the Wall. The large hilltop site has been partially excavated. The village outside the fort walls contains a dozen or more visible houses and building foundations. At one edge of the site is a reconstructed watch tower.

We climbed the Watch Tower at Vindolanda

We watched the crew dig up 2,000-year-old artifacts

"Can we climb it?" Emily asked.

"Yes."

Emily, Jessica, Gloria, Connie and I climbed to the second floor of the watch tower, while Linda explored the ground floor. She was still nursing her broken ankle. The second floor of the tower opened onto the top of the Wall. The reconstructors built the Wall with crenellated projections on the outer side to allow the defenders to hide behind those stones and shoot through the openings between the crenellations. No one is sure if Hadrian's Wall really had such crenellations, but they were common for that period. A narrow stairway led from the second floor up to the roof, where lookouts could scan the distant horizon looking for trouble.

Amy showed us a Roman post she had just dug up

"Can we go down to where they are digging?" Jessica asked, pointing to an archaeological dig by the wall of the fort.

"Okay," I agreed as we climbed down from the tower.

We walked down to the dig area and huddled close to the yellow tape barrier they had erected to keep visitors out.

"I wonder what they are looking for," Emily said as we watched a dozen workers wielding shovels, trowels, wheelbarrows and buckets.

"They're looking for anything the Romans may have dropped or thrown away: coins, weapons, pottery, clothes or bones," I said.

About that time, one of the diggers came over to the yellow tape carrying a bucket and a trowel.

She found bones, broken pottery, sandals and a skull

"Hi, I'm Amy," the young lady said. "Where are you from?"

"The United States," I said.

"Missouri," Connie added. "What are you finding?"

"This is part of a post," Amy said, holding up a four-inch square chunk of blackened wood about a foot long. "See the hole near the top? A cross member fit into that hole. And this is an animal bone, probably a cow's rib. Here is some broken pottery we found today."

"Are you an archaeologist?" Gloria asked.

"Yes," Amy replied. "I'm in charge of this team and the only paid professional. The rest of the team are volunteers, retired teachers, college students and housewives. We only dig during the summer months."

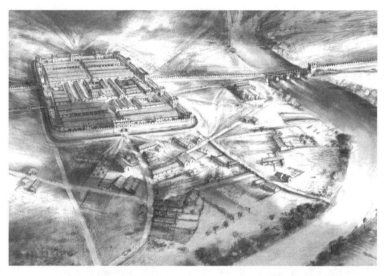

Artist concept of what a Roman fort looked like

"How long will it take you to complete the investigation of this site?" I asked.

"We've been digging at this site for about 36 years and at the rate we are going, it will take another 150 years to complete the excavation. Archeology is done very slowly and methodically. We don't want to miss anything. During the winter months we clean and catalog the items we found the past summer."

"Have you found any treasure?" Jessica asked.

"Yes, we consider everything we find to be a treasure," Amy said with a smile. "Yesterday we found a human skull. The day before we uncovered a gold earring and last week we found some gold coins. Our museum at the bottom of the hill has a great display of the kinds of things we've found."

"Thanks for taking the time to show us those things," Connie said.

It will take another 150 years to complete the excativation of the Vindolanda Fort site

"Would you like to come back next year and help us dig?" Amy asked the twins.

"Yeah," Emily said.

"You bet," Jessica seconded.

"See you next year," Amy said with a wave of her hand.

"The people are so nice over here," Connie said. "Imagine taking time from her work to talk to tourists and show us those things."

"Can we go down to the museum?" Emily asked.

"Good idea," I agreed.

We got back in the van and I started down the narrow, one-lane road to the museum at the bottom of the hill. The vegetation at the side of the road scraped both sides of the

89

One of the 2,000-year-old letters found at Vindolanda

van as we drove. Half way down we met a compact car trying to turn around. The driver had the car stuck between a tree behind and a fence ahead. After seven or eight back and forth maneuvers, the car finally got far enough off the road so that we could pass.

"I'm glad we didn't meet anything bigger than that little car," Gloria said as we drove into the museum parking lot.

The museum contained a fantastic collection of weapons, furniture, clothes, sandals, jewelry, pottery, coins, bones and paintings depicting life in Roman times. The most unexpected exhibit contained samples of over 2,000 documents written in Latin with pen and ink on wooden writing tablets. These tablets are the earliest archives of written material in British history. They included letters written by the senior officers and their wives; reports on military activities; and communications concerning food, clothing, supplies, buildings and transportation. One letter, probably to a soldier, recorded the sending of socks, sandals and underpants. Another was to the wife of the commanding officer at Vindolanda inviting her to attend a birthday party at a neighboring Roman fort. The documents provided an important insight into life on the frontier 2,000 years ago, including the price of beer. The majority of the letters have been moved to a special environment in the British Museum in London. That exhibit recently was chosen as the top treasure in the museum.

One of the paintings in the museum depicted the Roman toilet in the fort. It is hard to believe, but the Romans had flush toilets 2,000 years ago. The painting shows about two-dozen toilet stools around the room and a water source that ran under the stools to flush the waste away. The soldiers

The Romans had flush toilets and running water

used a sponge to wipe and then had a stream of flowing water in front of the stool to wash the sponge off. Another interesting observation about the toilet was the writing on the john walls. I always thought that illiterate misfits in the 20th century started the craze of writing nasty phrases on the john walls, but this writing is in Latin and since most of the soldiers couldn't read or write, it must have been written by the literate officers.

After touring the museum and eating lunch, we drove back up the narrow museum road.

"There's a big trailer truck coming down the hill," Gloria said about halfway up the hill. "Tell him to back up and let us out."

"I don't think there is any way he could back that thing up the hill," I said as I looked for a place to pull over. I had passed a barn a few minutes before and thought there might be room to pull off there so I started backing down the hill.

We walked the Bamburgh Castle grounds and toured the castle

Driving forward with a right-hand drive vehicle is one thing, backing up is another. I kept running off the road and having to pull forward to get back on it. Finally, I got down to the barn and was able to pull far enough off into the grass beside it to let the truck pass. I then pulled back on the road and hurried to the top before anyone else came down the hill.

From there we drove back to the east coast and headed north to Bamburgh Castle.

"Is this castle as old as the Roman forts?" Emily asked as we drove up to Bamburgh.

"No, the guidebook says the major part of the restored castle dates from the 1700s," I said, "but this has been a Royal center since AD 547. Most of what we'll see was rebuilt about

93

Bamburgh has been a Royal center for 1,500 years

250 years ago. It also says that Bamburgh is believed to have at one time been the castle of Sir Lancelot of King Arthur fame."

"Does anyone still live in the castle?" Jessica asked.

"Yes. The Armstrong family has owned the castle for the past 150 years and Lord Armstrong IV still lives here with his family."

"Can we go in and see where he lives?" Jessica asked.

"No. We can tour the downstairs of the castle," I said. "Lord Armstrong lives in the upstairs."

The first room we toured was the Crewe Museum Room. This 75-foot by 50-foot room had a 40-foot high ceiling.

"It must cost a fortune to heat this place," Linda said, looking at the immense expanse.

"And they did it with fireplaces," I added.

We examined the Crewe Museum Room

We walked past exhibits of armor, dinner service, part of the foundation of Hadrian's bridge over the Tyne River from Newcastle, school chairs dating from when the castle was a school and dozens of paintings. Most of our group took a brief glimpse of the exhibits and continued on to the next room. Emily stood by herself in front of a painting of a knight fighting a dragon.

"Are you ready to go?" I asked her.

"No. I'm trying to read the story of the dragon," she said, pointing to the stylized English text around the edge of the painting.

"Can I help you?" I asked.

"Yes, please do."

"Once upon a time there was a King of Northumberland whose Wife died leaving him with one Child, good and beautiful, a Maiden of eighteen named Margaret, beloved alike by Court and People.

Soon afterwards a dark Woman of the wild Land-in-the-west fascinated the King so they married and he brought her to the Castle of Bamburgh where a royal Feast was spread in honor of the Homecoming.

Margaret ran to meet them at the Gate. The Queen greeted her with Kisses and a smiling face, But she was really jealous of her Beauty and soon determined to be rid of so dangerous a Rival.

One Day therefore she invited her to come and see some Jewelry in a private Chamber and no one being near transformed her by Witchery into a strange Beast which fled roaring from the Castle.

It made its Lair among the Crags and from thence roamed abroad Blasting the Trees with its Breath and

The painting related the story of the Laidley Worm

devouring the flocks for miles Around and soon was known as the Laidley Worm of Spindlestone Heugh.

Its fame spread far and at last reached a young Knight, Childe Wynd, who determined to free the Peasants from so grievous a Plague so he set Sail and the wind being Fair soon reached Bamburgh.

Now the Queen being on the Watch Tower saw the Ship afar and knowing why it came hastily sent a Man-of-War to destroy it, But Childe Wynd's crew was victorious and sunk the Queen's Boat with all on board.

The Laidley Worm stood raging on the Cliffs and by its terrible Breath drove them out to sea again. Finding no means of landing, the Ship was run for Budle Bay and the Crew safely gained the Shore.

Childe Wynd then left his Men and followed the now retreating Beast. He overtook it among the Crags of

Spindlestone and had raised his sword to strike when with Eyes full of Tears, it piteously cried out.

Telling him its Story and how the Spell of Enchantment could only be removed by his kissing it thrice before the Sun had sunk behind the Hills and that if he did not the Spell would bind forever.

The Knight stooped down and kissed the loathsome Worm, its Scales turned dim, it withered, dried, burst into flame and the Princess Margaret rose from the Ashes, more Beautiful than ever before.

Childe Wynd wrapped her in his Cloak, placed her on Horseback and together they made their Way to Bamburgh. Their coming was already spread abroad and the People ran joyfully to meet them.

The King was glad to see his Daughter but the Queen was sorely afraid and kept to her Chamber. There Childe Wynd sought her and by her own Arts turned her into a Toad.

Childe Wynd and Margaret married and on the death of the King they sat together on the Throne surrounded by their Children and ruled over a peaceful and contented People."

"That's a nice story," Emily said as we left the room looking for the rest of our group. They had gone through the rest of the castle without us and were shopping in the castle gift shop.

"Did you see the ghost?" the guide asked a group of school children in the gift shop that had just completed their tour.

"No," they mumbled. "What ghost?"

"A long time ago one of the Armstrong daughters had a tragic love affair," the guide began. "Her father disapproved of the boy she was in love with and sent the unfortunate suitor overseas for seven years. He forbid the couple from exchanging messages and hoped that his daughter's passion would cool. The young woman became more and more depressed. In a desperate attempt to persuade his daughter to forget her lover, the father told her that his spies discovered that the boy had married someone else abroad. However, to cheer her up after this devastating news, the father directed the castle seamstress to make a fine dress in his daughter's favorite color—pink. The distraught daughter donned the finished garment, climbed the stairway to the highest tower, and flung herself to her death on the rocks below. Shortly afterwards her lover returned from his exile, unmarried, and heartbroken by her death. Ever since then, the daughter's ghost, clothed in a dress of shimmering pink, wanders through the corridors of the oldest section of the castle before gliding down the rocky path that leads to the beach. There she stands upon the sands, gazing sadly out to sea, forever awaiting the return of her lost love. We've had several visitors tell us they encountered the ghost while touring the castle," the guide said. "That's a likeness of her painted when she was seventeen," the guide said pointing to a large painting on the wall behind the cash register.

Emily and Jessica bought pens at the gift shop that light up when you write with them. Gloria bought books (including the Armstrong ghost and dragon stories) and everyone bought postcards.

We stopped in the castle teashop for supper. Soup, sandwiches and, of course, ice cream. At bedtime, Gloria read several dragon stories to Jessica and Emily.

Chapter 10

Robin Hood's Tree

"I think I'm recovered enough to drive today," Connie said at breakfast. On our drive to Housesteads, we scared up two cock pheasants as we passed near the village of Twice Brewed.

"Twice Brewed is an odd name for a town," Connie said. "I wonder how it got that name?"

"I don't know," I said. "Why don't you stop for tea at a pub near here and ask?"

We parked in the Housesteads parking lot and everyone walked into the gift shop. The girls/ladies wouldn't miss an

Near Housesteads we could walk on top of the Wall

A long section of Hadrian's Wall extended west from Housesteads

opportunity to shop. "That's half the fun of travelling," Connie said. I bought books, maps and snacks for our hike.

"We'll meet you in the car park at the Walltown Quarry," I told Connie, circling the meeting place on her map. "There's a Roman Army Museum nearby so turn right when you see the sign to the Museum."

"You mean we have to climb that hill again today?" Jessica complained. "We climbed up here two days ago."

"Two days ago we turned right and walked back to Chollerford," I explained. "Today we'll turn left and walk to Walltown."

"How come we are always going uphill and never get to come back down?" Emily asked as we trudged up the steep hill.

A section of doorway arch at Milecastle 37

"We go up and down," I said. "It's just the lay of the land."

"It sure seems that we have a lot more uphills than down," Emily complained. Jessica agreed with her.

"There's a bunny," Emily shouted as a brown rabbit darted across the path ahead of us.

"And another rabbit," Jessica said as a little rabbit ran after its mother.

"There's two more," Emily said pointing down a path to the left. A mama rabbit and her young hopped down the path away from us.

We climbed up, past the Housesteads fort and to the Wall. This was the one place where we were allowed to walk on top of the Wall. The top of the six-foot high Wall was

The Wall zigs and zags to follow the cliffs

covered with dirt and a thick crop of grass. We climbed on top of the Wall and headed west. We didn't meet as many tourists this day as we met the last time we started at Housesteads, just a few hikers.

The path followed the edge of the crags up and down really steep hills. In some places they had placed limestone blocks as steps on the slippery hillside. Emily and Jessica ran on ahead of me and I had to hustle to keep up with them. The six-foot-high Wall continued unbroken for several miles. The area around Housesteads is lightly settled and the local farmers apparently didn't steal stones from the Wall for their houses or fences.

The only visible indication of Milecastle 37 is part of the Roman arched gateway in the north wall. The top of the

We had some steep climbs down the cliff faces

archway is missing, but the three curved courses starting about four feet above the ground are quite distinct.

As we came to the end of Hotbank Crag, we had a great view of Crag Lough (Lake) ahead of us. A substantial two-story stone cottage overlooked the lake. We sat on the stone fence by the cottage and ate our snack while drinking in the fantastic view: brilliant green grass running down the hill to the sparkling blue lake; white sheep grazing in the field; the black, rocky Highshield Crag rising 400-feet high behind the lake and Hadrian's Wall visible along the top of the crest.

"It doesn't get much prettier than this," I told the twins.

"I think this is the part of Hadrian's Wall I'll remember best," Emily said. "It's looks like a fairytale."

"I'd like to live in that house," Jessica said.

The crags all face north with a gentle slope to the south

"Me too," I agreed.

We climbed the hill to the top of the crag. A strong wind blew across the lake from the west.

"Look at those birds," Emily said, pointing to several big, black crows flying into the wind. "That looks like fun." The crows flew at the same speed the wind blew so they appeared to stand still over the lake. Periodically one of them would shoot upward, turn a flip (an aerial maneuver called an

Hadrian's Wall clings to the edges of the crags

Immelmann) and glide downwind. Then it would turn around and fly back upwind to where the other crows were hovering.

Emily and Jessica kept running ahead of me

We watched them for ten minutes while they cavorted in the wind.

"What kind of birds are those" Jessica asked, pointing to two white swans sitting at the west end of Crag Lough.

"They're wild swans," I said. "It looks like they are sitting on their nest." I tried to get a photo of them, but when they put their head down they just looked like a white blob. One would raise its head and then put it down when the other swan raised its head. Finally both birds raised their heads at the same time and I snapped the photo. People ask why it takes six or seven hours to hike 12 miles. It's because we spend half of our time looking at things and the other half hiking.

This part of the walk reminded Emily of a fairytale

As we climbed down Sycamore Gap, a depression between two crags, we came to Robin Hood's Tree and King Arthur's Well.

"Why do they call it Robin Hood's Tree?" Emily asked.

"This 70-year-old tree got its name when Hollywood decided to use it as the backdrop for the film, 'Robin Hood, Prince of Thieves' staring Kevin Costner," I explained. "The first 20 minutes of the film takes place around this very tree. And that well is called King Arthur's Well," I said pointing to a stone well 50-foot from the tree. "It was in the movie too."

"Let's eat lunch here," Emily suggested.

I took the cheese, crackers, yogurt, carrots, apples and cookies out of my backpack. We ate and relaxed in the shade

We stopped for lunch by Robin Hood's Tree

of Robin Hood's tree. While we sat there, about 20 young, noisy hikers ran down the hill from the west.

"There goes the neighborhood," Emily said as the kids continued to jabber, drop candy wrappers on the ground and act obnoxiously. Fortunately they didn't stop at Robin Hood's Tree, but continued up the other side of the crag.

A little further along we came upon Milecastle 39, also known as Castle Nick because it was built in a natural nick in the hills between two crags. This is the best-preserved milecastle along the Wall. The 10-foot thick castle walls are about 6-foot high and 30-foot long on each side. Six or eight building foundations are clearly visible inside the castle and wide gateways on the north and south walls allows passage

This tree was featured in the movie "Robin Hood - Prince of Thieves"

through the castle. About 30 soldiers would have been stationed in the two-story milecastle.

Emily and Jessica found coins by Milecastle 39

As I rested on the castle wall, Emily and Jessica busied themselves exploring the inside of the castle and digging around in the dirt.

"I found a coin!" Emily said excitedly, holding a small, worn, brass coin up for me to see.

"Me too," Jessica yelled, holding up a slightly larger brass coin.

"Can we keep them?" Emily asked.

"They're pretty worn," I said, examining the coins. "I can't read anything on either side of them. I doubt if the officials would care if you kept them."

"Yea," Emily said as she and Jessica put their newfound treasures in their pockets.

We stopped often for a snack and rest

We hiked on to Cawfield Quarry, one of the many the Romans dug. They quarried one million stones for the face of the wall and several times that amount of rubble to fill the ten-foot section between the faces. Clear, cold water filled the abandoned quarry. While I sat and rested by the side of it, Emily and Jessica skipped stones on the sparkling, blue water. Jessica couldn't equal her 22-skip record set back in Whitley Bay, but she could usually get a respectable 6 or 8 skips each time.

As we walked by a farmhouse on the other side of the quarry, a friendly, golden cocker spaniel started following us. When we came to the stile over the fence we expected the dog would stay on the farm side, but it wiggled under the

The twins skipped stones on the Roman quarry

fence and continued on with us. At the next stile, it ran up the steps and over the top to keep up with us.

"Do you think the dog is going to get lost following us?" Emily asked.

"I don't think so. It acts like it knows the way pretty well."

It followed us across the fields, over hills, through the woods and across roads. As we passed two other hikers, the man asked, "Is that your dog?"

"No, he just followed us," Jessica said.

"You mean you're dognappers?" he said with a laugh.

"We tried to get it to go home, but it keeps following us," Emily said. And follow us it did. I started pointing a finger at it and ordering it to go home. The dog would lay

A golden cocker spaniel followed us for hours

down for a minute and then get up and follow us. We passed a sign in a sheep pasture stating, "Loose dogs are in danger of being shot!" This dog never bothered the sheep, but just kept following us. I tried again and again to get it to go back. Finally we were able to disappear around a turn in the woods and the dog didn't follow.

As we came to a stile next to a woods, Emily and Jessica played a trick on me. They had already crossed the stile and before I crossed, Jessica turned and asked, "Grandpa, what kind of tree is that?" pointing behind me. I turned around and tried to figure out what kind of tree it was. "I don't really know," I said, "probably a beech." When I turned back around, the girls had disappeared into the woods. I caught up with

The girls loved to see the little lambs

them a few minutes later and they were still laughing about tricking me.

"Why are all these dead moles hanging on the fence?" Emily asked as we passed a fence with a dozen moles draped over the barbwire.

"I understand there was an old custom here for the gamekeeper of the land to hang the dead moles on the fence to show the landlord that he is doing his job of keeping the population of the destructive moles down," I said. "Some farmers still do it out of pride."

We arrived at the Walltown Quarry parking lot and saw the van, but couldn't see Gloria, Connie or Linda.

"I'll run down to the lake and see if they are there," Jessica offered. I sat down in the grass while Emily and Jessica went looking for our group. About five minutes later the whole gang came walking back from the lake.

"We didn't think you'd be here so quickly so we went sightseeing," Connie said. "How was your walk today?"

"Great," Emily replied. "Jessica and I found old Roman coins by the castle."

"Really," Connie said. The twins dug the coins out of their pockets and showed them to Connie, Linda and Gloria.

"You girls are really lucky," Linda said.

"Today we hiked along the prettiest part of the Wall so far," I told them. "Did you find out about the origin of Twice Brewed?"

"No," Linda said. "We asked, but no one seemed to know the answer."

"How would you like to go swimming?" I asked Emily and Jessica on the drive home.

"In the ocean?" Jessica asked.

"No. Haltwhistle has a heated pool in town."

"Yeah," the twins agreed. "Only, I didn't bring my swimming suit," Jessica said with a frown on her face.

"I've got an extra one," Connie said. "Let's see if it will fit you." Jessica tried it on when we got back to the hotel and it did fit when they pinned the back straps together.

The Haltwhistle Leisure Centre has a heated outdoor pool. The changing room is coeducational, but there are individual cubicles with doors for people to change in privacy. We got into our swimsuits and walked outside to the pool. The air temperature was cool, about 65°F, but the water was warm, 84°F. Emily and Jessica played at the deep end, turning underwater somersaults and doing handstands while I swam laps.

"I'm cold," Emily said after about 30 minutes of playing in the pool so we got out, dressed and drove back to the hotel.

After supper I worked on my trip journal while Gloria read. About 8 o'clock Emily knocked on our door.

"Donna is on TV!" Emily said excitedly. We turned the TV on and saw our friend from Dayton, Donna Fontaine, on a program called Wife Swap. About eight months before the trip Donna had been chosen to film this Wife Swap reality program. She had moved in with some other family for a week and that family's wife took Donna's place in her home in Dayton for the week. Naturally, the producers chose two totally different types of families to make the swap more interesting. Donna has four children and her family is totally kid-oriented. The other family had a single daughter and the family was career-oriented. The father was a very successful businessman and the mother a successful real estate salesperson. They had a house manager, cook, maid and tutor/ companion for the daughter. The husband and wife never arrived home by suppertime so the family never ate together. The first thing Donna did was to fire all the help and demand that the family eat supper together every night. The other wife didn't know how to cook and about went crazy trying to prepare meals for a big family, do the laundry and pick up after four kids. In one scene, the wife is shown lying on her back in the grass in front of Donna's house with a beer in one hand trying to recover from a hard day of housework. Gloria and I hadn't seen the show in Dayton since we don't have cable TV. We had to come to Haltwhistle, England, to watch Donna's performance.

At the end of the TV program, I walked outside to enjoy the evening air. A white-haired gentleman sat in the

117

courtyard across from our bungalow. He had his pipe in one hand and a glass of wine in the other, alternately drinking and smoking.

"Beautiful evening," I said.

"Yes it is," he agreed. "Are you here to walk the Wall?"

"Yes. My grandchildren and I started at Wallsend and plan to walk the whole Wall."

"I walk a section of the Wall every year," he said. "I used to work on the canals and rivers in the Cambridge area. It was my job to schedule the maintenance on the locks and right-of-way."

"When did you retire?" I asked.

"About 14 years ago," he said between puffs on his pipe.

"What section are you walking this year?"

"I think I'll walk from Housesteads to Birdoswald tomorrow. That's one of the prettiest sections of the whole Wall," he said.

"We walked from Housesteads to Walltown Quarry today and plan to walk to Birdoswald tomorrow," I said. "Perhaps we'll see you on the trail."

"Perhaps."

Chapter 11

You Need to Use More Nouns, Grandpa

"The town used to be called 'Alt Thistle'," Grace, the hotel owner's wife told us when I asked about the origin of the town name. "I think that is Celtic for 'high place above two rivers'," she said. "The name changed several times and was eventually standardized when the railroad came through. They published a time schedule and Haltwhistle became the official name. I think they liked that variation because it sounded more like standard railroad terms than the other variations."

I drove the van to Walltown Quarry where Emily, Jessica and I planned to start our walk.

"We'll see you in Walton about 4 o'clock this afternoon," I said as Connie slid into the driver's seat.

"Have a good walk," Connie called out as the three ladies waved to us.

We started walking along a deep section of the vallum. I would have thought that during the intervening 2,000 years, it would have filled up with mud and debris, but it still had the sharp V shape of the original dig. The fields along the vallum were full of sheep and lambs. Emily made us weave back and forth to avoid walking too close to the lambs.

"We don't want to scare the poor little things," she said.

A middle-aged lady with a big overnight pack on her back struggled up the hill toward us.

"That looks like a heavy pack you're carrying," I said.

Ruins of 14th century Thirlwall Castle

"It is," she replied, breathing heavily. "Eighteen kilos (40 pounds) and it seems to get heavier each day."

"Are you hiking the entire length of the Wall?" I asked.

"Yes. I hope to do it in seven days," she said. "That's all the holiday I have."

"I like your walking stick," Emily said, commenting on the handsomely-carved hiking stick the lady held.

"It belonged to my father," the lady said with a smile. "He carved it from an oak sapling out of our garden many years ago."

"Good luck on your walk," I said as we started down the hill.

"May the wind be to your back and the trail down hill," she replied as we parted.

"What's that?" Jessica asked as we came upon ruins at the top of the next hill.

"According to the placard, it is the Thirlwall Castle, a four-story structure with five story towers built by John Thirlwall in the early 1300s" I read to Emily and Jessica. "It's made entirely from stones taken from Hadrian's Wall. It repelled attacks from unwelcome visitors during the Anglo-Scottish border raids in the 15th and 16th centuries. Peace and stability came gradually during the 17th century—but too late for the castle. Abandoned by the Thirlwall family, the castle began to attract a new type of visitor——families of birds, bats, insects and plants all made their homes within its crumbling walls. And there is a Thirlwall legend. It says that during one raid, the family hid their most prized possession, a small gold table, down a deep well where it remains to this day, protected by a magic spell."

"Is that another one of the hidden treasure stories like the oxen in the lake?" Jessica asked.

"I'm afraid it is," I confessed.

As we left Thirlwall Castle, we passed a barn where the sheep were crying.

"Baaaa, baaaa, baaaa, baaaa," they cried loudly.

"I wonder what's wrong with the sheep," Emily said.

"They're probably going to get shorn and don't like being confined," I answered.

The field behind the barn contained a big herd of cows. Most of them were black with a white stripe around their belly. A few of the cows were reddish brown and a few gray, but they all had the wide white stripe around their belly. I've seen hogs colored like that, but never cows. My friend Hannah said they are a rare breed called Belted Galloways.

The black cows had a white stripe around their middle

"Are we going to see any of the Wall today?" Emily asked late in the morning.

"I think we will," I replied.

"I'll bet we don't," Emily said.

"Okay, I'll bet you a pound we see the Wall today," I said as a challenge.

"Okay, a pound," Emily agreed.

About 30-minutes later, we reached the village of Gilsland and found a section of the Wall and part of Milecastle 48 on the outskirts.

"You owe me a pound," I told Emily.

"Hold out your hand, Grandpa," she said.

I did and she poured a pound of rocks in my hand.

"You need to use more nouns, Grandpa," Emily said with a laugh.

The Wall path took us through beautiful gardens

I didn't think fifth-grade Emily knew what a noun was!

"That's a pretty bridge," Jessica said, pointing to a high, single arch railroad bridge over a little stream.

"The Romans taught us how to make that kind of arch," I said as we walked under the bridge to examine it.

"These look like strawberries," Jessica said, pointing to wild strawberries growing under the bridge.

"They are."

"Can I eat them?" Jessica asked.

"Yes." We stopped, picked and ate the small, sweet, wild strawberries.

Thirty minutes later we stopped for a snack and to put more sunscreen on our faces. Jessica poured a big puddle of sunscreen in the palm of her hand just as a Royal Air Force jet

Emily bet we wouldn't see any of the Wall this day
came screaming over, 100 feet above our heads. Jessica
instinctively slapped her hands over her ears. As she took her
hands down, I could see she had an ear full of sunscreen. I
used my hankie to wipe the sunscreen off her neck and out of
her ear.

"At least my ear won't get sunburned," Jessica said,
always looking on the bright side of things.

We met an elderly couple hiking from the other
direction, stopped and introduced ourselves.

"We're from the Netherlands," the lady said in slightly-
accented English.

"My granddaughter and I rollerbladed 700 kilometers
around Holland with backpacks," I told the couple. "We chose
Holland because it is so flat."

"That's why we have come here for holiday--because it is not so flat," the lady said with a laugh.

A little further along the path we came to the remnants of the Roman Willowford Bridge across the River Irthing. The river has changed course since the bridge was built and now runs about 50 feet west of the ancient abutment. A new arched steel bridge now crosses the river. While we were looking at what appeared to be the remnants of a water powered mill by the bridge, a group of about 25 German tourists came from the other direction and crowded around the base of the bridge. Their guide gave them a lengthy explanation of the history of the bridge in German. I could understand enough of the German to follow the sequence of events. The tour group had come from the Birdoswald Castle, a mile beyond the bridge.

We continued on to Birdoswald and met Gloria, Connie and Linda in the gift shop there. Where else would they be? Connie had met a couple from Dayton in the gift shop and brought them over to talk to us. They lived in Englewood, a few miles north of Dayton and were vacationing in England with their two small children. It is a small world!

I stamped our Wall passports in the gift shop. We now had four of the six stamps.

We ate our lunch at picnic tables in the castle courtyard and then went outside to take photos. I took a photo of Gloria knitting on the wall surrounding the castle. We had heard the following story of a farmer knitting on the wall and discovering a cave with a bewitched King Arthur.

A farmer from Sewingshield was sitting knitting on the ruins of Birdoswald Castle by Hadrian's Wall when his clew (ball of yarn) fell and ran downward through a rush of

Gloria knitting where the farmer found King Arthur's cave

briars into a deep subterranean passage. Full in the faith that the entrance into King Arthur's hall was now discovered, he cleared the briary portal of its weeds, and entering a vaulted passage, followed in his darkling way, the thread of his clew. The floor was infested with toads and lizards; and the dark wings of bats disturbed by his unhallowed intrusion, flitted fearfully around him.

At length his sinking faith was strengthened by a dim, distant light, which, as he advanced, grew gradually brighter, till all at once, he entered a vast and vaulted hall. In the center of the hall a fire without fuel, from a broad crevice in the floor, blazed with a high and lambent flame. The firelight showed all the carved walls, and fretted roof, and the monarch and his queen and court, reposed around in a theatre of thrones and costly couches.

On the floor, beyond the fire, lay the faithful and deep toned pack of thirty couples of hounds; and on a table before it the spell dissolving horn, sword and garter. The shepherd reverently, but firmly, grasp the sword, and as he drew it leisurely from its rusty scabbard, the eyes of the monarch and his courtiers began to open, and they rose till they sat upright. He cut the garter; and as the sword was being slowly sheathed, the spell assumed its ancient power. The King and court all gradually sunk to rest (the shepherd was supposed to cut the garter and blow the bugle to break the spell); but not before the monarch had lifted up his eyes and hands and exclaimed,

"O woe betide that evil day,
On which this witless wight was born,
Who drew the sword-the garter cut,
But never blew the bugle-horn!"

Emily and Jessica were excited about exploring the castle ruins to try and find the cave. Their favorite game is hide-and-seek and they were sure they could find the hidden passage if it was really there. They searched all around, but never found the cave.

"Sounds like another one of Grandpa's tall tales," Emily concluded.

The twins and I started walking again as Connie and the ladies drove off for Walton. The path flattened out with only an occasional small hill. Most of the fields held grazing sheep, not crops. Several trains passed by headed from Newcastle to Carlisle. Emily and Jessica waved to the passengers in the silver two-car train and some of the

127

One of the many "kissing gates" we encountered

passengers waved back. We met no other hikers after Birdoswald.

"That's a big wall," Emily said as we stopped to look at a 30-foot-long section of the Wall. This section stood at least 10-feet high, the highest section we had encountered so far.

"There's a bunny hopping toward us," Jessica said, pointing to a big, brown rabbit hopping down the road toward us. When it got to within 10-feet, it turned abruptly and hopped into the bushes at the side of the road.

"I thought it was going to run us over," Emily said.

As we approached Walton, a cloud of blackbirds flew over us and landed in the trees on both sides of the road. They all seemed to be chattering at the same time making a

Connie wanted a photo of her in the right-hand drive van to show her friends back home

deafening racket. We steered clear of the trees as we walked into Walton. Connie had parked the van by the pub so the ladies could use the facilities if they needed. I took a photo of her in the right-hand driver's seat for her to show her friends back home. Then we loaded our backpacks in the van and I drove on to Carlisle looking for our hotel, The Angus. Carlisle is one of the oldest cities in England, dating from before the birth of Christ. We made two passes through the twisty streets of downtown Carlisle, but couldn't find the hotel. On the third pass I stopped by a taxi zone and asked one of the cabbies where The Angus was.

"Make a left at the top of the hill," the cabby said. "Go straight across the traffic circle, across the river and up the hill. It'll be on your right-hand side at the top of the hill." British taxi drivers have to pass a comprehensive test to get their taxi license and they know the cities they drive in. We followed the cabby's directions and pulled up to The Angus Hotel five minutes later. I pulled into a short-term parking lot near the hotel, parked and went in to make sure we had rooms. The clerk gave me the three room keys and I went back to the van. As we unpacked the luggage, Emily walked over to the car parked next to us and picked up a £5 note from under the front end of the car.

"Can I keep it?" Emily asked.

"Yes, dear," I said. "Finder's keepers, loser's weepers."

"All I ever find are pennies," Jessica complained.

It started raining hard as we carried the luggage to the room. It seemed amazing that it had never rained as we walked, only a few hours of light drizzle one day.

Every night I checked Emily's and Jessica's feet to see if they had any blisters or sore spots. Fortunately they never did. The new boots and socks we bought before the trip fit very well and were worth the money.

The hotel had a nice Bistro on the ground floor so we chose to eat there that night. They had delicious fresh grilled salmon with a bournaise sauce, broccoli, cauliflower, baked potato and salad. The twins chose ice cream for dessert naturally, but the adults opted for double chocolate devil's food cake, "wickedly rich."

Chapter 12

Don't Mess Around With a Curse

"Ahhhhh!" Emily yelled when the cashier dropped and broke her strawberry pushup candy. We had gone to the nearby grocery after breakfast to get snacks for the day.

"Go back and get another one dear," the cashier advised her.

"There aren't any more," Emily said with a frown on her face. "We looked for one for Jessica and there aren't any more." She picked out a Fruit Rollup to replace the broken pushup.

I bought cheese, yogurt, carrots, apples, bananas, oranges and some snack crackers to munch on during our hike.

I drove the van back to Walton where the twins and I started our walk. Gloria, Connie and Linda got out of the van for good bye hugs and waved to us as we disappeared down the path. It was a perfect day for a walk--sunny, warm and a cloudless sky. Emily and Jessica skipped along the path singing nursery rimes while I hustled to keep up with them. About a half-hour into the walk we headed up a steep, grassy hill when I felt something bulky in my right pant's pocket. I don't usually carry anything in that pocket, so I stopped to investigate. **IT WAS THE VAN KEY!**

"What are you going to do?" Jessica asked as I stood there in shock.

"I guess I'll run back to the van and give them the key," I said.

"Can we stay here?" Emily asked.

"Yes, you and Jessica stay right here. Don't move from this spot until I get back," I said as I slipped off my backpack, laid it down in the grass and started jogging back up the path. I jogged all the way back to the van.

"It's about time you came back," Connie said as I jogged up to her. "We were about ready to ride down to try and meet you on the Wall path."

"How were you going to do that?" I asked.

"A lady came by walking her dog a little while after you left and she offered to go get her car and drive us down to the next town," Connie said. The lady drove up and parked in front of the van as we were talking.

"It's okay," Connie said. "He came back with the key. Thanks for the offer."

"Glad to help," the lady replied as she drove off.

"I was going to try to run and catch you after we discovered the key was missing, but you had already disappeared by then," Gloria said.

I figured we had gotten almost to Newtown when I discovered the key so we drove to Newtown and I walked back up the path from there. Emily and Jessica were waiting about 500 yards from the Newtown road.

"You should have walked slower, Grandpa," Jessica said. "We're not done playing." They were stripping the seeds from the tall grass and filling Jessica's hat. "Can we stay a little longer?" she asked.

"No, I think we had better be moving on," I said. "You can collect the grass seeds as we walk." We walked toward Newtown, passing a pasture with a thoroughbred mare and her colt. They were frolicking around, racing from one side of the field to the other. A sleek stallion pranced around in the adjacent field. He trotted over to the fence and whinnied. The mare stopped running and looked around. He whinnied again and the mare took off at a full gallop toward the fence with the colt trailing behind, trying to keep up. The mare and stallion rubbed necks and neighed to each other while the colt tried to join the love-in. We walked carefully along the edge of the field so we wouldn't get run down by the horses.

Connie and the van were still in Newtown when we got to the road.

"Have a good walk," Gloria yelled to us as we crossed the Newtown road.

The sky became cloudy as we stopped to rest and to put on another application of sunscreen.

"My friend's dad laid outside for five hours on a cloudy day and got a real bad sunburn," Jessica said. "He had to go to the hospital."

"You're right," I said as I applied the sunscreen on my neck. "You can get a sunburn even on a cloudy day."

"Are we nearly there?" Emily asked.

"No."

"Are we half way?"

"No."

"Are we half way to half way."

"Yes, I think we are half way to half way," I said with a laugh.

We came to a boggy area in the woods. Someone had used split logs to outline the trail, positioning the logs so the sharp edge of the split pointed up. Emily, Jessica and I walked on them and balanced ourselves by holding onto nearby trees to get over the muddy part of the trail.

We stopped for lunch under a shady tree

"Let's sing," Emily suggested when we reached the dry part of the path.

"Row, row, row your boat,
gently down the stream,
merrily, merrily, merrily, merrily,
life is but a dream."

"Let's each start the song when the other person gets to the end of a verse," Jessica suggested.

"Row, row, row
your boat gently   row, row, row
down the stream; your boat gently   row, row, row
merrily, merrily   down the stream; your boat gently
merrily, merrily;   merrily, merrily,   down the stream;
life is but a dream. merrily, merrily; merrily, merrily,

life is but a dream.   merrily, merrily;
                          life is but a dream."
   "Merrily, merrily, merrily, merrily," Emily got confused
and followed Jessica's part of the song. We tried several times
to get through the whole sequence and never made it. Someone
would always join in on someone else's verse. After that,
Emily and Jessica sang their DARE song and Bah, Bah, Black
Sheep. Then they made up a song that went;
   "I miss mommy, I miss her so, I really do.
   "I miss Kelsey, I miss her so, I really do."
   The song continued for 10 minutes while they
substituted the names of their cats, dog, hamster, classmates,
neighbors, teachers and cousins for mommy.
   We stopped to eat lunch under a huge shade tree in a
grassy pasture.

The hedgerow contained dozens of kinds of wildflowers

In the village of Old Wall we saw the Old Wall Cottage

"What is that foam on the grass?" Jessica asked, pointing to a half-inch diameter blob of white bubbly foam on the stem of a tall plant.

"I don't know," I said. "I thought it might be slobber from a cow, but there are too many of them around here to be random slobber. Write that question down in your journal and ask your teacher this fall when you start school," I suggested.

As we started out after lunch, we passed a farm and saw hundreds of automobiles on car carriers parked by the barn. "I wonder why they have all those cars there," Emily asked.

"Another good question for the teacher," I joked.

Nine cats came out of the cottage door

As we walked, Emily and Jessica continued to gather grass, strip the seeds off and put them in Jessica's hat.

"What are you going to do with all those seeds?" I asked.

"This!" Jessica said as she raised her hat and dumped all the seeds on her head.

"That's cute," I said as I helped her brush the seeds out of her hair.

As we got to the village of Old Wall, we passed a beautiful white stone house named Old Wall Cottage.

"Look at the cat," Emily said as a tiger-striped cat came out of the open front door of the cottage. Emily and Jessica knelt down to pet it. Then another cat came out of the

The long-haired jackass bellowed for attention

cottage, and another, and another, and another until nine cats lined up by the girls to be petted.

HEEEE HAWWWWW, HEEEE HAWWWWW, a long-haired jackass brayed from the pen next to the cottage. It appeared to be upset that the cats were getting all the attention. It stopped braying when I walked over to the pen and scratched its neck. Emily and Jessica felt sorry for the jackass so they came over and gave it some attention. Then they went back and played with the cats. It took 30 minutes for the girls to play with and scratch all nine cats. As we started to leave, a small, gray whippet (looks like a greyhound) came out of the cottage with its tail between its legs. The girls had to pet the dog before we could continue our walk.

The girls played with the cats for 30 minutes

At Bleatarn Farm we encountered a small, low section of Hadrian's Wall, the only section we saw all day.

The clouds cleared and the sun came back out. It became hot, without even the hint of a breeze. So much for the predicted cold, rainy weather. Emily and Jessica skipped down the path, singing, giggling and having a great time. We met three bunny rabbits and a big brown dog on the path. The bunnies hopped away, but the dog came over to have his belly scratched. From the top of the hill we could see the tall buildings in Carlisle.

"We don't have far to go now," I told them.

After crossing the highway, we stopped by a farm field with a sign warning, "Beware of Bull," and shared an orange. Then we walked into High Crosby and stopped at the pub for ice cream. You might get the idea that our walking is secondary to our eating. That is probably true for Emily and Jessica. We continued on to Linstock, eating our ice cream on the way. As we got near the car park where we were to meet Connie, the girls broke into a run, rounded the corner and ran all the way to the van. They seem to have an inexhaustible supply of energy.

When we arrived back at the hotel, I stopped by the desk and asked Rachael, the desk clerk, about the cars we had seen stacked up at the farm.

"They're from the flood," Rachael said.

"What flood?"

"Back in January we had a lot of rain and the river flooded the whole downtown," Rachael replied. "The water was up to the tops of the lamp posts down at the traffic circle. Over 5,000 cars were destroyed in the flood. A lot of them have already been shipped away for salvage. Those you saw are waiting to go."

"Does it flood often here?" I asked.

"No. It has been hundreds of years since it flooded like that," Rachael said. "Some people say it happened because of the curse."

"What curse?"

"The Carlisle City Council commissioned a local artist to develop an ancient curse as part of the millennium artwork," Rachael said. "The artist, Gorden Young, fashioned a 14-ton granite boulder and inscribed the 300-word curse. The infamous curse originated back in 1525 when the Archbishop of Glasgow developed it to try to stop the cross border families, known as reivers, from stealing cattle, raping and pillaging. It was designed to frighten the lawless people of the Anglo–

The Carlisle City Council authorized the Cursing Stone

Scottish borders. It excommunicates the 'common traitors, reivers and thieves,' dwelling in the Scottish Middle and Western Marches of the Anglo-Scottish Border. Specifically, it curses 'their head, their hands, their feet, their legs, their bowels, their stomach and their heart.' The curse promises they would suffer in Hell unless they 'forbear their sins and make satisfaction and penance.' Since the Cursing Stone went on exhibit in 2000, the livestock herds in this area have been wiped out by hoof-and-mouth disease, a huge fire destroyed a full block downtown, Carlisle had the worse flood in 200 years, several factories have gone bankrupt and closed their doors, a boy was murdered in a local bakery and the Carlisle football (soccer) team played so poorly that it has been dropped from the league. People are talking about destroying the Cursing Stone to keep anything else bad from happening."

"It's a good idea not too mess around with curses," I said.

"That's right," Rachael agreed.

Emily, Jessica and I had met an English lady, Hannah Grove, in Canada when we went on the Willmore Horseback Adventure in 2003. She worked as one of the wranglers taking care of the horses with the Wild Rose Outfitters. I contacted Hannah when I started planning our walk and asked her to join us. She worked six days a week so the only day she could walk with us was Sunday. Hannah took the train from Edinburgh to Carlisle and I met her at the train station at 11 PM Saturday night and drove her to our hotel.

"How was the train ride?" I asked.

"Long and tiring," Hannah said. "I slept most of the way."

"You're in room five," I said, handing her the key. "We'll see you at 8 o'clock for breakfast."

"Good night," she replied.

Chapter 13

Cuckoo Spit

"I want some Toxic Waste," Emily said, putting the candy on the counter of the grocery store.

"Ultra sour-flavored candy made from nuclear sludge," I read on the candy label. "Created deep in the Secret Laboratory of Professor Sauernoggin. Best if eaten before July 1, 2010."

"Are you sure this stuff is really edible?" I asked.

"Oh, yeah, it's great," Jessica said. "We've had it before. It's reeeealllllyyyyy sour!"

We bought more cheese, crackers, fruit and yogurt for the day's snack.

When we got back to the room, Gloria and I went for a walk before breakfast. It was a beautiful morning with the golden sun shining through the trees, the birds chirping and the sweet smell of the blooming flowers in the neat English gardens.

"This is an Unadopted Street and may not be used as a car park," the sign read on a small side street.

"I guess that is what we call a private road," I said as we headed back to the hotel for breakfast.

"I don't think I'll be able to drive the van through Carlisle today," Connie said at breakfast. "There is too much traffic and the route is too confusing. Is there some way you can get a ride back from your end point today?"

"I'm sure there is," I said. "We'll figure it out."

After breakfast I drove Emily, Jessica and Hannah to Linstock and dropped them off at our starting point, the car park. Then I drove back through Carlisle and out to Burgh-by-Sands, our end point for the day. The village appeared completely deserted, no sign of life at all. It didn't have a store, gas station, shop or anything except one pub and about 50 houses. I parked the van by the "Greyhound Pub" and knocked on the locked front door. No answer. There were a dozen cars in the pub parking lot, but still no answer when I pounded again on the front door. As I was about to give up hope of finding a ride, a man came out of the house directly across from the pub and got in his truck. I hurried over and approached the driver's side.

"Good morning," I said. "Could I use your phone to call a taxi? I need a ride back to Carlisle."

"There're no taxis out here," the man said. "One would have to come out from Carlisle. I'm headed that way and would be glad to give you a ride to town. Hop in."

I ran around to the passenger's side and got in. "I'm Allen Johnson from the United States," I said. "My grandchildren and I are walking Hadrian's Wall and I wanted to drop our car here since this is where we'll end up this afternoon."

"I'm Joe Sealby," he replied, extending his hand for a shake. He had the firm grip of a man who works with his hands.

"What kind of work do you do, Joe?" I asked as he started down the road toward Carlisle.

"I'm a steel fabricator," he answered. "See those steel outbuildings on that farm?" he said, pointing to a big shed in the nearby field. "I'm in charge of the gang that erects those buildings. I've got a meeting this morning with our company representative from our plant in Birmingham to go over our schedule for the next few months. The company salesmen visit the farmers and sell the buildings. Then my gang goes out and erects them."

"Were you born around here?" I asked.

"No. I was born on the other side of Carlisle and moved to Burgh-by-Sands about five years ago."

"Were you affected by the big flood?" I asked.

"Not out in Burgh, but Carlisle was devastated," Joe said. "Thousands of cars were destroyed, hundreds of businesses and at least a thousand homes. The flood occurred this January and some of the people won't be back in their homes until Christmas, a full year. I'm headed downtown for my meeting. Where can I drop you?"

"I'll get off at the traffic circle," I said. "I read about the cursing stone. Do you think they should remove the curse?"

"I don't really believe that a curse can cause a flood, but just the same, it's nothing to mess with," Joe said. "I'd be for getting rid of the stone if they asked me."

"Thanks for the ride, Joe," I said as he pulled over to the edge of the traffic circle and let me out.

"Have a good walk," Joe said as he drove off.

The traffic circle was about two miles from Linstock. Rather than trying to hitch another ride, I decided to jog back to Linstock. I started down the biking path alongside the River Eden. I met a number of people out for a Sunday morning walk with their babies in a pram or their dog on a leash. There were even a few joggers and the occasional bicyclist. It took me about 30 minutes to jog to Linstock. When I arrived at the car park, I found Hannah giving a horticulture lecture to Emily and Jessica.

"She knows the names and uses of all the plants," Emily said as we picked up our backpacks and started to walk back to Carlisle.

"Maybe Hannah can answer some of the questions you had, like why do the moles dig so many holes in the ground," I said.

"They have to dig a lot of holes to aerate their tunnels," Hannah replied. "It's the same thing the Underground (subway) does in London. They have to build ventilation shafts every mile or so along the tunnel."

"How come people hang the dead moles on the fences?" Emily asked.

"It's sort of a show of pride or skill," Hannah said. "The moles dig lots of tunnels in the fields and the cows or sheep can break their legs if they step in those holes. So the farmers set traps for the moles and when he catches them he hangs them on his fence to display his trophies."

"What is the foam we see on the plants, like that stuff?" Jessica said, pointing to a blob of foam on the stem of a tall plant.

"Oh," Hannah said with a laugh, "we call it cuckoo spit. It's a secretion that an insect called a froghopper makes by blowing air into the sap of the plant. Apparently they use it to protect themselves until they are large enough to hop away. The mature froghoppers are sap-sucking insects about the size of a match head. They don't seem to cause any harm to the plants so most people don't spray them or try to get rid of them. Let's see if we can find the larvae in the spit." Hannah took a blade of grass and dug around in the frothy foam. As she probed around in the white mass, a little black blob about

1/8 inch long appeared and started climbing up the blade of grass.

"If you look real close," Hannah said, holding the blade of grass up, "you can see the little froghopper."

"He's not very big," Jessica said. "I wonder how something that small can blow all those bubbles."

"Persistence," I said.

Hannah buried the froghopper back in his foam on the plant and we continued our walk.

"Why do the bullfighters wave a red cape to make the bull mad?" Emily asked.

"Bulls are color-blind," Hannah said, "so it doesn't matter to them what color the cape is. The bull sees the motion of the cape and that is what makes him mad. The red-colored cape is to impress the spectators."

"You were working at a pony farm, training the animals the last I heard." I said. "Are you still working there?"

"No," Hannah replied, "a pony threw me and I broke my arm so I moved to Edinburgh last winter. Now I have to work three jobs to pay the rent: clerking for a chemist, waiting tables and washing dishes."

"I've got something on my arm that itches," Emily complained. She had a dozen big welts on her arm.

"You must have brushed up against some nettle," Hannah said, pointing to a tall plant with hairy leaves that grew next to the path. "Try not to touch it. Those tiny hairs on the leaves cause a nasty burn." Hannah looked around in the weeds near the path until she found the plant she wanted, broke a leaf and rubbed the sap on Emily's blisters. They stopped itching immediately and the welts disappeared in about 10 minutes. The lady has an amazing knowledge of nature.

Jessica, Hannah and Emily on the River Eden Bridge

"I make nettle tea in the spring," Hannah said. "I use only the small, tender leaves near the end of the plant and wear heavy gloves when I pick it. The tea is quite medicinal."

"Look at that bug," Emily said.

"It's a millipede," Hannah replied, rolling the bug over on its back with a twig. "See how the legs move in a wave, all coordinated." A wave rippled down the upstretched legs as it tried to right itself.

We crossed the River Eden on a stone footbridge, stopping in the middle of the bridge to watch the river. A placid stream of water flowed lazily underneath. "This was a raging torrent last winter," Hannah said. "The flood water was 5 meters (16 feet) above this bridge."

As we reached the other side of the bridge, a small, brown mouse ran across the dirt path.

"I think that was a dormouse," Hannah said. "The Romans used to eat them."

"Ugh!" Jessica exclaimed scrunching up her nose at the thought of eating a mouse.

"They fattened them up on nuts, stuffed them with mince and cooked them," Hannah continued. "Quite a delicacy. Some of the country pubs in this area still have dormice on their menu."

"Remind me not to eat there," Emily said.

"We were talking about moles earlier this morning," Hannah said. "They used to make moleskin gloves in some of the shops in Carlisle years ago. They were very comfortable and fashionable, but they are not made commercially any more."

A cluster of elephant-ear plants grew along the walk by the river. The leaves of the rhubarb-like plants grew three feet in diameter.

We came to the Sands Sports Centre, in the middle of Carlisle and went in for lunch. I stamped our passports and ordered drinks for lunch. We had cheese, crackers and yogurt in our backpacks.

"Ahhhhh," Emily said as she opened her backpack. Her yogurt had spilled out and was all over the inside. I took it to the restroom and cleaned it out. Then we ate our lunch and ordered ice cream for dessert.

We left the Sands, crossed under the traffic circle on the river walk and continued toward Burgh-by-Sands. Emily and Jessica ran to a playground next to the river and started swinging. Hannah and I stopped by the chinning bar.

"Can you chin yourself?" Hannah asked as she chinned herself several times.

"Yes, I think so," I said as I pulled myself up a couple of times. "I have to double-up my legs to get started."

"So do I," Hannah admitted. "I don't understand how that helps, but it does."

Emily and Jessica came over to the bar and tried. Neither twin could chin herself. I thought all children could chin themselves. They can swing across the ladder bars, but they couldn't chin themselves.

We came to an old bathtub in the field that the farmer probably used as a water trough. Emily and Jessica posed for a photo by it, laughing about not having any privacy for their bath in the middle of a farmer's field.

As we walked on, Hannah picked some cow parsnip flowers that looked like Queen-Anne's lace and rubbed them on her clothes. "That'll keep flies away," she said.

"What are these flowers?" Jessica asked, pointing to some big, daisy-like white flowers with a yellow center.

"Those are ox daisies," Hannah said. "And these are speedwell," she said pointing to little blue, forget-me-not like flowers. "They feed them to race horses to make them run faster. Do you like butter?" she asked Emily.

"Yes," Emily replied.

"Let's see," Hannah said as she picked three buttercup flowers. She held the buttercups under Emily's chin and her neck glowed bright yellow from the reflection of the shiny petals. "Yep, you do."

"There's a butterfly," Jessica said, pointing to a black butterfly with orange and yellow wings.

The bathing facilities in Carlisle are a bit primative

"And some white ones," Emily said pointing down the trail. We had seen very few butterflies on our walk, but at least a dozen beautiful butterflies fluttered around us now.

"This must be a butterfly bush," Hannah said.

"You mean butterflies grow on a bush?" Emily asked in amazement.

"No," Hannah replied with a laugh, "the flowers on the bush attract butterflies."

"Ouch!" Jessica yelled. She had been eating carrots from her snack pack and had bitten her thumb. "I've got sharp teeth," she reported.

"What are the pretty purple flowers?" Emily asked.

151

"Those are foxglove," Hannah said. "The dried leaves are used to make digitalis, a powerful heart medicine and diuretic."

"Did you ever make a wristband note pad?" Hannah asked me as I jotted notes in my little notebook and put it back in my shirt pocket.

"No, I never did, but it would be a good idea," I said. When the twins and I were horseback riding in Canada with Hannah, I kept taking my notebook out of my pocket as we rode, jotting notes and trying to put the pad back in my pocket without falling off my horse. Hannah mentioned she had read where a naturalist had attached a notebook to a strap and secured it to his arm so it would be handy when he wanted to jot notes or draw a plant. Such a device would be handy for me since I'm constantly writing notes while I'm bicycling, riding a horse or camel or canoeing.

As we walked along the River Eden, we frequently came to small clearings by the river with a camper parked at river's edge. It seems that many British families spend an inexpensive holiday camping by the river where the children can swim, fish or boat. The shore was mostly sandy and the water clear, making a nice private swimming beach.

"They may be migrant or gypsy families, we call travellers, who move about the country in their caravans looking for work," Hannah suggested.

Further down the river several crows were wading in the shallow water, cooling their feet while half a dozen sea gulls floated lazily down the stream.

"What's that sweet smell?" Jessica asked as we passed a clump of flowers.

"That's clematis," Hannah said. "They have an overwhelming sweet fragrance."

"Look at the wind blowing the grass in that field," Emily said pointing to a huge field of wheat across the river. The local wind caused waves to ripple through the wheat from one end of the field to the other. Sometimes the waves traveled along the river and sometimes at an angle, depending on the direction of the wind.

As we rested by the side of the trail and ate our snacks, an English couple came by and stopped to chat.

"How much of the Wall are you walking?" the lady asked.

"The whole thing," Emily replied proudly.

"Are you enjoying the walk?" the man asked.

"Yes," Jessica replied. "We've seen lots of animals and flowers and old stuff."

"That's great," he said. "We're part of the volunteer patrol. We are responsible for keeping the litter cleaned up on a three-mile stretch of the path, checking the signs and noting the condition of the trail."

"It's funny," the lady said, "we traveled to Canada for a holiday last year and our friends there took us to see a 200-year-old wall in Montreal. I didn't have the heart to tell them that we live by a 2,000-year-old wall."

We started walking again and as we passed through Beaumont, Jessica lagged behind. Emily, Hannah and I stopped at the edge of the village to wait for her to catch up. She came running down the path with a handful of clover.

"Look at all the four-leaf clovers I found," Jessica said breathlessly. She had 10 four-leaf clovers in her fist.

Jessica found a patch of four-leaf clover in Beaumont

"Can we go back?" Emily asked. "I want to find a four-leaf clover."

"Okay," I agreed. We walked back to the corner house and all started looking through the clover. There were dozens of four- and five-leaf clovers. Everyone found them including Hannah.

"I've never found a four-leaf clover in my life," Hannah said excitedly. "This must be a toxic waste dump to have so many mutations in one spot." We ended up with about 25 four-leaf clovers. As we hunted through the clover, a group of four hikers walked briskly past us, turned the corner and continued the way we had come. A few minutes later, a distraught-looking lady came jogging down the path.

"Have you seen a group of four hikers?" she asked.

Emily and Jessica disappeared in the root system

"Yes, they passed a few minutes ago," I said. "Just turn the corner and follow the path."

"I went off the path for a potty stop and when I came back, they had left me. I haven't any idea where I'm going," she said as she trotted on to catch her group.

"I've been looking forward to your visit for over a fortnight," Hannah said as we continued on.

"What's a fortnight?" Emily asked.

"It's two weeks," Hannah replied. "The word 'fortnight' is really a contraction of fourteen nights. There is also a sennight for seven nights or a week from old English, but that isn't used anymore.

We came to a giant beech tree, probably 1,000 years old, with a tangle of roots protruding from the ground. The roots had a small opening at ground level and without hesitation, Emily and Jessica dropped their backpacks and squeezed into the hole under the roots. They disappeared into the bowels of the 10-foot diameter tree.

"What if there is a bear or raccoon or snake in that hole?" Hannah asked.

"I guess the bear will have to fend for himself," I replied.

The girls played in the roots for about 10 minutes and then we continued on to Burgh-by-Sands. We stopped at the Greyhound Pub for ice cream.

"Do you know Joe, who lives right across the street?" I asked the bartender as he served us the ice cream.

"Sure," the bartender said with a laugh. "He's right over there playing pool."

I walked over to the pool table and shook hands with Joe. "These are my grandchildren and my friend, Hannah Grove," I said. "And this is the man who gave me a ride this morning."

"How was your walk?" Joe asked Emily.

"Great," Emily replied. "We saw lots of butterflies and found a bunch of four-leaf clovers."

"It was a fortunate coincidence that I met Joe this morning and got a ride back to Carlisle," I said as we drove back to the hotel.

"I don't believe in coincidences," Jessica said. "I believe it was God's plan."

"You're probably right," I agreed. "Too many good things have happened to us to be just random coincidences."

When we arrived back at the hotel, we picked up the ladies and drove to the Guzzling Bridge Pub for fish and chips. After supper, we took Hannah back to the train.

"I wish you could do the whole walk with us," Emily told Hannah. "You know a lot more about the country and nature than Grandpa."

"I wish I could too," Hannah said. "But I have to go back to work."

"I love you," Jessica said as she hugged Hannah.

"I love you all," Hannah said as she got on the train and waved good-bye.

Chapter 14

King Arthur's Camelot

"Yea!" Jessica yelled. "Today is the last day of walking."

"I'm not ready for it to be over," Emily said. "I'm having too much fun."

We drove the van to Bowness to find a place to meet at the end of the walk.

"This car park is near the end of the Wall. Let's meet here," I suggested.

"Okay," Connie agreed. "It's on the only road through town so I think I can find my way back to it."

Then we drove back to the Greyhound Pub. Emily, Jessica and I got out and started our walk. There were a few more people in Burgh-by-Sands Monday morning. We passed a house that had a wrought iron sailboat design built into their gate. I stopped to get a photo while the twins continued to walk together along the road. They passed a man and a woman chatting alongside the road.

"Are you lost?" the woman asked Emily.

"No, we're walking Hadrian's Wall," Emily replied.

"By yourself?" the woman asked.

"No, with our Grandpa," Jessica replied. "He's back there taking pictures," she said pointing back down the road.

"Have a good walk," the lady said.

When I caught up with the twins, Jessica suggested we whistle instead of singing. The three of us walked along whistling for the next 15 or 20 minutes. The bright blue sky, warm sunshine and cool breeze made us feel happy and carefree. It doesn't get much better than this!

After we stopped whistling, Jessica made up a song about marching. It went on for a full 15 minutes. When Jessica finally stopped, Emily commented, "I didn't know a song could be that long."

"Yes, a song can be pretty long," I said. "In the olden days there were entertainers called balladeers who entertained in the taverns or inns. Their songs often consisted of the unwritten history of a king or stories of knights and fire-breathing dragons. A single song could run 30 minutes or more."

We walked along an abandoned railroad bed that ran alongside the road.

"It's odd that the cows follow this path (as evidenced by the frequent cow paddies on the path)," Jessica said. "I wonder why they don't cross the road."

"I guess they don't have anywhere else they would like to go," I replied. "They don't like to go to the movies or watch TV because they can't understand the words."

"Maybe they would if someone put in subtitles in moo language," Emily suggested.

"If we could teach one cow to understand what we were saying, then she could interpret the movies into cow language," Jessica said.

"We'll have to work on that when we grow up," Emily concluded.

"That's Scotland in the distance," I said, pointing across the river flowing parallel to the road.

"Could we walk across to Scotland?" Jessica asked.

We stopped to explore the tidal flats

"It's pretty muddy in those tidal flats along the river," I said.

"Maybe we could ride a cow across the river," Emily suggested. "Can cows swim?"
"Yeah, they can swim," I said, "but I think it would be pretty uncomfortable riding the bony back of a cow."

"Can we walk down to the edge of the river?" Jessica asked.

"Good idea," I said. We crossed the road, climbed over the fence and walked across the field of tall grass to the tidal flat. The river had cut a three-foot high sheer drop at the high-tide edge of the field. We hopped down the embankment and walked across the dry, sandy bank. The tidal flat must have been half a mile wide at this point with only a 100-foot wide stream flowing down the center to the Irish Sea at low tide. We came to another abrupt drop in the land with several tidal pools.

"Look at the fish swimming in the water," Emily said, pointing to minnows swimming in the pool.

"There's a crab," Jessica said. She used a sea gull feather to poke the motionless crab. It skittered off sideways to get away.

The girls explored the tidal area finding shells, bones, pretty rocks and sea gull tracks. Jessica found some flat shale rocks. "These are Skipper's friends," she said as she put the shale in her backpack. Skipper was the rock from Whitley Bay that skipped 22 times.

"Can we eat lunch?" Jessica asked.

"Okay," I said. "Let's cross the field and get back to the path first. We sat in the sun by the side of the path and ate our lunch. There were no trees or shady spots in sight, just flat grassy fields.

"Do you realize that we have been going downhill all day?" I asked Emily. She had complained that we always go uphill and never get to go back down. "We'll go from 100-feet above sea level down to sea level today, with no uphills."

"It looks like we are just going along level," Emily said. "I don't think we are really going downhill."

After lunch we walked into the village of Bowness. I expected a big "End of Wall" sign, but we didn't see anything indicating where Hadrian's Wall ended. We continued to the center of the village and stopped at the King's Arms Pub.

"Where is the end of Hadrian's Wall?" I asked the bartender.

We walked into the village at the end of Hadrian's Wall

"Go two blocks back up the street and turn left," he said. "You can't miss it."

"We already missed it once," Emily said, "I hope we don't miss it again and have to walk all the way back to the hotel."

"Do you have passports for me to stamp?" the bartender asked.

"Yes," I said, digging them out from my backpack.

He stamped them and gave us each a beautiful certificate verifying we walked the wall. Then we walked back up the road and found the little wooden shed with signs for the end of the walk. I positioned my camera on a post, set the timer and ran back to get in the photo of us under the "End of Hadrian's Wall Walk" sign.

Collect your stamps on the way...

If a stamping station was unavailable, the Hadrian's Wall Information Line will stamp your passport for you.

STAMPING POINT: Segedunum Roman Fort &
Museum - Start of Trail, GR: NZ 301 661
SITUATED: Inside main entrance of museum
WHEN AVAILABLE: Normal opening hours
Additional Stamping Station: TOTAL Petrol Station,
150 yds east of Segedunum Roman Fort.

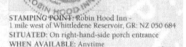

STAMPING POINT: Robin Hood Inn -
1 mile west of Whittledene Reservoir, GR: NZ 050 684
SITUATED: On right-hand-side porch entrance
WHEN AVAILABLE: Anytime

STAMPING POINT: Chesters Roman Fort &
Museum - (Chollerford), GR: NY 911 704
SITUATED: Inside and outside main entrance of
museum
WHEN AVAILABLE: Standard English Heritage
opening hours (Outside box available out of hours).

STAMPING POINT: Birdoswald Roman Fort - 1.5
miles west of Gilsland, GR: NY 615 663
SITUATED: Inside and outside main entrance & shop
WHEN AVAILABLE: Normal opening hours (Outside
box available out of hours).

STAMPING POINT: Sands Sports Centre - Carlisle,
GR: NY 402 565
SITUATED: Inside main entrance to centre - access
via glass door from riverside path.
If locked access at front of building
WHEN AVAILABLE: Normal opening hours

STAMPING POINT: The Banks Promenade or The
King's Arms - Bowness-on-Solway, GR: NY 223 628
SITUATED: At the very end of the Trail
WHEN AVAILABLE: Anytime - The Banks
Normal opening hours - The King's Arms

Name _____

Address _____

_____ Postcode _____ Phone _____

We had our passports stamped at the six way stations

I'm going to have my shoes bronzed and hang them on my wall

"I'm so proud of myself for walking the whole thing," Jessica said, "that I'm going to have my shoes bronzed and hang them on the wall by my certificate."

"I'm proud of both of you girls," I said. "You walked 100 miles of rough trail. That's quite an accomplishment."

"Can we do it again?" Emily asked with a laugh.

"NOT!" Jessica said.

We walked back past the King's Arms and down to the car park where we found Connie, Linda and Gloria talking to the local bus driver.

"The driver has to wait until 3:30 PM before he starts on his route so we've been talking to him while we waited," Connie said.

"He told us how 'Once Brewed' and 'Twice Brewed' got their names," Linda said. "He said 'Once Brewed' was a village that didn't allow liquor to be served, just tea. The beer drinkers all moved down the road and established a town that allowed beer. They called it 'Twice Brewed' because of the beer fermentation process."

"How was your walk?" Gloria asked the twins.

"Good," Emily replied. "We didn't have to walk up a single hill today."

"Look what I found," Connie said as she laid out a colorful collection of broken pottery and dishes. "I walked along the bank of the river and found these pieces sticking out where the tide eroded the bank. They were buried two or three feet below the surface so they must be old."

Emily and Jessica were fascinated with the broken pottery. They tried to match like-colored pieces to see if they could reconstruct a bowl or pot. There weren't enough pieces to make a complete anything, but they enjoyed trying to fit the puzzle together.

Since it was still early, I suggested driving back to Walton to try to find a Roman fort reputed to be the site of King Arthur's Camelot.

"Your Grandpa and I visited Tintagel in Southwestern England a few years ago. It is supposed to have been the birthplace of King Arthur," Gloria told the twins. "He lived at around the end of the 5th century. King Arthur married Guinevere, the most beautiful maiden in the land. He and his knights of the round table protected the common folks from the barbarians of the north who robbed and pillaged England. They say Arthur was mortally wounded in a battle along Hadrian's Wall and his knights took him to an island where his half-sister, Morgan Le Fay, lived. She had special skills in the art of healing and they hoped she might save him. It isn't clear whether she saved him or not, but his legend lives on."

The guidebook shows a Roman fort called Camboglanna about two miles west of Walton. The book says this is one of the sites that historians think might have been Camelot. I stopped at the pub in Walton and asked about the site, but no one there knew anything about it. Driving down the road near where the site appeared on the map, I found a single-lane dirt farm road leading across the field to a big stone mansion set back in the woods. The lane had a locked gate so it appeared we couldn't get there that way. The guide book showed a back road behind the mansion so we drove to Newtown and turned down a single-lane gravel road back toward the mansion. That road passed the Beck Farm and finally petered out in a farmer's barnyard at Cambeckhill.

"I'd like to explore the woods to see if I can find the remains of the fort," I said.

"We'll wait for you," everyone else volunteered.

I had a detailed topographic map that showed a path and bridge leading across the stream and up to the Roman fort. I found the path and crossed a narrow walking bridge. On the other side, I found stone steps leading up the hill. The woods was full of pink flowering rhododendron bushes and some other white flowers. Near the top of the hill, I passed several small, square grassy clearing that looked like picnic areas except there were no tables or facilities. As I approached the mansion, I heard a rustling in the woods ahead of me. I froze and stopped breathing. A pair of small brown deer walked down the path, stopping to eat as they moved toward me.

The deer finally realized I was there and took a leap into the underbrush at the side of the path. I continued up the hill and stopped when I heard voices. Peering through the woods I could see a man and woman working in the garden behind the stone mansion. A large mastiff-type dog sniffed around the garden a few feet from the couple. I decided to turn around at that point and walk back to the car rather than try to outrun the dog. I had the definite feeling that this could have been Camelot. The quiet woods, beautiful flowers, cool grassy clearings, deer feeding by the trail and tranquil brook provided an idyllic Camelot-like setting.

"Did you find Camelot?" Connie asked when I arrived back at the car.

"Yes, I think I did."

Emily ordered strawberries with sweet cream for dessert following supper at the hotel. She loves strawberries.

"How were the strawberries?" I asked.

"Great," Emily said, licking her lips. "I should have ordered them every night instead of ice cream."

Chapter 15

Crepe Suzette in London

"I want small," Emily said.

"I'll take a large," Gloria said.

I was taking orders for "I Walked the Wall" T-shirts for all six of us. I finally located the shirts at the Tourist Centre in downtown Carlisle. Then we took off for London. We picked up the M-6 Motorway outside of Carlisle and headed south. The green, hilly countryside was beautiful. This Lake District is a favorite holiday spot for city-bound Londoners. Emily and Jessica played "I Spy" for the first part of the trip and then slept.

We pulled off into a Comfort Stop about noon and went in to eat.

"Look at the doggy dishes," Jessica said. The complex had a dish of dog food and a dish of water near the front door for the dogs. A lot of Europeans travel with their dogs. They even allow dogs in most restaurants.

We ate at Burger Chef so the twins could get their fast-food fix. They had been eating real food for two whole weeks. After ordering, we all sat down and they brought our food to the table. When the twins finished their chips (French fries) with tomato sauce (catsup) we continued on toward London. We picked up the M-1 Motorway near Birmingham and followed it in to the North Circular Road. We were headed for Hyde Park on the west end of town and I was sure there would be signs as we neared central London. NOT! I followed signs to Central London and ended up on the east end of town, nowhere near Hyde Park. No problem, I thought. Just follow

Holburn Street west until it becomes Oxford Street and that would take us right by Hyde Park. As we reached Holburn Street I saw it had been turned into a bus and taxi only street—no private vehicles. No problem, we'll just go a block further and find a parallel street to follow over to Oxford. There are no parallel streets in London. Everything radiates out from squares or circles (circus). Trafalgar Square, Oxford Circus, Piccadilly Circus, Marble Arch and Victoria Station, we saw them all as we followed one-way streets all over London.

"Are we lost, Grandpa?" Jessica asked.

"No, dear," I said. "I'm just giving you a brief tour of London."

"We've passed that monument with the big lions three times so far," she noted.

"I wanted you to see Trafalgar Square from all different directions," I said.

We eventually found the Wellington Arch and drove up the east side of Hyde Park. Our destination, the St. David's Hotel, was on Norfolk Square near Paddington Station. After a two-hour tour of central London we finally arrived in front of our hotel. A block-long row of identical, white, five-story Edwardian houses had been turned into tourist hotels. A row of parking meters lined the street in front of the hotel. Fifty pence for 12 minutes. That's £2.50 per hour (about $5.00 per hour at the June 2005 exchange rate). I parked there long enough to check in and then moved the van to an underground long-term parking lot at Paddington Station. We planned to take public transportation to get around the city. I had done enough driving around London to last me for a year.

We had two triple rooms in London in place of the three twins in our other hotels. Emily roomed with Gloria and I while Jessica bunked in the room with Connie and Linda.

"I'm hungry," Gloria said as we hauled our luggage up to our third floor room. We all walked around the corner to the Alhamba Steak House. Gloria and I had eaten there on previous visits to London and liked the service and food. After a delightful meal, Emily and Jessica ordered ice cream with fresh strawberries. I decided to splurge and ordered crepe suzette. A few minutes later the waitress brought my plate of thin French pancakes covered with syrup and a huge blob of whipped cream. As she took my crepe suzette off the serving tray, she made a big sweeping motion with it like throwing a Frisbee and the crepe flew off the plate and landed in Linda's lap.

"Ahhhh!" Linda yelled looking down at the mountain of gooey whipped cream in her lap.

"Oh! I'm so sorry," the red-faced waitress said, mopping the whipped cream off Linda's lap with cloth napkins. "I'll bring another crepe suzette. You can have your slacks cleaned and send us the bill. Would you like a complimentary dessert, ma'am?"

"No thank you," Linda said.

The crepe suzette tasted great, but it sure caused a lot of trouble.

It started raining really hard and lightning after we went to bed. I got up to close the window and saw a man sleeping on a bench in the park across the street from the hotel. He lay curled up in a fetal position, getting soaked, but he never moved. The lightning came crashing down and the thunder woke Emily. She doesn't like lightning.

170

"I can't sleep," she said.

We talked about the walk and her cats at home. Then I read her a story from the book about dragons. By the time I finished the story, the lightning had stopped and Emily went back to sleep.

"I almost got squashed during the thunderstorm last night," Connie told us in the morning. "Jessica and I were lying in bed watching TV when a bolt of lightning hit right outside our window. Linda was standing by the bathroom door and she jumped three-feet high and landed in the middle of our bed, right between Jessica and me."

The hotel provided a great breakfast: bacon, eggs, fried tomatoes, toast, a choice of hot or cold cereal, orange juice, half grapefruit, coffee, tea and milk. While we ate, the hostess came around to check on us.

"Is there anything else we can get you?" she asked.

"No, thank you. This is great," Emily said.

A little later the chef came out in his tall white hat and made the rounds of the tables.

"Was your breakfast cooked to your taste?" he asked.

"Yes, thank you," Jessica said. "I like your hat."

After breakfast I walked to the newsstand and bought all-day bus passes, £3.00 for adults, £1.00 for children. They don't make change on the bus; you have to have exact change or a bus pass. When I got back to the hotel, I hailed a taxi and the six of us headed for Harrods, the premier department store in London. Connie, Linda, Emily and Jessica went off looking for souvenirs while Gloria and I went up to the book and magazine section. Gloria found a mystery novel to read on the airplane flight home and a couple of knitting magazines.

171

We rode the double-decker bus to Westminster Abbey

"Can you find out where the restrooms are?" Gloria asked me.

"Where is the nearest restroom?" I asked a sales lady hurrying up the aisle wearing a Harrods' nametag.

"I haven't any idea," she replied in an irritated manner. "I don't even know where I am," she muttered as she hurried on. I searched around a little and finally located the restroom for Gloria.

Then we wandered back down to the toy floor and found Emily and Jessica watching a four-foot-high animated stuffed monkey and six-foot-high giraffe perform.

"Can we buy them?" Jessica asked.

"I don't think so," I said. "We'd have to buy them a seat on the airplane to get them home."

172

They ended up buying small teddy bears wearing a British flag vest. Then we went up to the cafeteria and ate ice cream along with a piece of cherry pie.

We left Harrods and walked to the Knightsbridge bus stop.

"Can we go upstairs?" Jessica asked as we got on the double-decker bus.

"Yes," I said. We were the only passengers on the upper deck. Emily and Jessica sat in the front of the bus and pretended they were driving. We changed buses at Victoria Station and got off at Westminster Abbey.

"This is a big church," Emily said as we walked into the Abbey and she looked up to the 75-foot-high ceiling.

"This church is over 1,000 years old," I said, reading from the guidebook. "The Abbey was founded in 960 as a Benedictine monastery. It has been the site for the coronation of all the Kings and Queens of England since 1301. This was also where the funeral of Princess Diana took place in 1997." We toured the Abbey, stopping to read about the knights and kings buried there and to view the magnificent works of art. Then we went to the gift shop and bought postcards.

We took the bus back to the hotel, changing at Covent Garden.

"Look at the men on the white horses," Jessica said pointing out the window. The Royal Horse Guard trotted along the street on their way from their barracks to Buckingham Palace. They were dressed in red uniforms with silver-plumed helmets. We got off the bus at Paddington Station. Gloria and Linda decided to rest in our hotel rooms, but Connie and the twins wanted to shop some more. I took them to a souvenir store and they bought T-shirts with pictures of London on them, postcards, magnets with London sights and London key rings.

For supper we went to Aberdeen Angus Steak House. This night we chose chocolate fudge cake and Peach Melba for dessert--decadent. After supper, Linda and Connie went on a Jack the Ripper nighttime tour. Emily, Jessica and I watched Brazil and Argentina play football (soccer) on TV for the Empire Championship. Brazil won, 4 to 1.

"We got to see where the murders occurred," Connie said when they got back at 10:30 PM.

"The tour took us back to the time of the murders," Linda said. "It was eerie being in the same spots that is part of history. I had the sensation of being there when it happened. I sat on the bench where Catherine Eddows was found dead. The guide said I was sitting where her head was. It was real spooky, exactly what I was hoping for."t (See Appendix E for more information on the Jack the Ripper Tour).

Thursday morning Gloria, Emily, Jessica and I drove south to Portsmouth to visit a dear friend. Connie and Linda planned to tour a cemetery in London and shop for the day.

I met Stan Stannard in 1974 when I attended a technical meeting in Ottawa, Canada. The U.S., Britain, Canada and Australia governments formed "The Technical Cooperation Program" (TTCP) after World War II to share military technology. Stan worked for the Royal Naval Laboratory at Portsmouth, England, and I worked for the Air Force Research Laboratory at Wright-Patterson Air Force Base in Dayton, Ohio. Gloria and I saw Stan at the TTCP meeting several times a year and established a lasting friendship with him and his wife, Doreen. Every time we get to England, we stop to

174

The Spinnaker Tower at Portsmouth is 558-feet high

visit them. Stan retired in 1987 and Doreen died several years ago, but we still visit Stan when we are in England.

"My, how the twins have grown," Stan said when we arrived in Portsmouth. "Your grandfather sends me pictures of you so I've watched you grow from babies to young adults. Your sister, Kelsey, and cousin, Tracy, stopped to visit me a few years ago when they came to England to have tea with the Queen."

We spent several enjoyable hours talking about military technology, children, grandchildren and world events.

"Our Portsmouth Spinnaker Tower is £12 million over budget and 6 years behind schedule," Stan said, pointing out the window at the sail-shaped tower in the distant harbor. "It wasn't supposed to cost the taxpayers anything, but as usual we are getting stuck paying for their incompetence and mistakes." (Four months later, in October 2005, Stan sent me two newspaper articles about the grand opening of the Spinnaker Tower: **"Spinnaker lift jam spoils opening day,"** from the Portsmouth Journal and **"I'm the project manager, get me out of here,"** from the Daily Telegraph. It seems that the state-of-the-art external elevator on the 558-foot-high, £36 million tower broke down on opening day with the Spinnaker project manager, the chief engineer from the company that built the lift and an engineer from the company that built the tower. They were trapped in the elevator for almost two hours while the opening day crowd of tourists and international media watched from below. The article noted that there was no toilet in the lift and since the walls and floor were made entirely of glass, the trio had no opportunity to relieve themselves.

Stan served us a delightful lunch of quiche Lorraine, pork pie, bean salad, slaw and topped off the meal with ice cream and cookies for dessert.

Late in the afternoon we drove back to London, picked up Linda and Connie and drove to the Quality Hotel Gatwick so we would be close to the airport for our flight home early Friday morning. The hotel had an indoor swimming pool, which was the main selling point as far as Emily and Jessica were concerned. "I'll sleep on the floor if necessary so we can stay at a hotel with a heated swimming pool," Emily said.

Emily, Jessica and I changed into our swimsuits and raced to the pool before supper. We played "Marco Polo" where the "it" person closes his eyes and calls out "Marco." The other players answer "Polo" and the "it" person staggers blindly about trying to catch the fleeing Polo answerer. I never could catch the twins when I was "it," but it was good exercise chasing them. We swam until suppertime.

"We had a great day at the cemetery," Linda said at supper "We took the subway up there and caught a bus back."

"We stopped at a bakery for lunch," Connie added. "We ate fresh, warm bread, soup and a kidney pie. It was delicious."

Chapter 16

Building Wonderful Memories with Family

I laid in bed unable to sleep Thursday night thinking of all the neat things I'd experienced during the previous two weeks; hiking with the grandchildren, touching Hadrian's Wall, watching archaeologists dig up 2,000-year-old artifacts, eating in quaint country pubs and **BAMM**, it was morning.

We drove to Gatwick Airport early, worried about how long the security check would take. There we checked in, walked to the departure lounge and had a fellow passenger take a photo of our whole group.

"I'd like to get everyone's impression of the adventure while it is still fresh in your minds," I said as I took out my notebook. "Let's start with Jessica."

"The funniest thing that happened was when Grandpa thought the boy with long hair was a girl," Jessica said with a laugh. "The most exciting was when we met Aunt Connie and Linda at the airport on the way to England. The most interesting thing was seeing parts of the Wall. I touched it and it felt really old. The hardest part was climbing up and down all those hills on our 12-mile hikes. The most unusual thing was the 20-minute rain that flooded our street at our first hotel and the waterfalls on the steps leading to the beach. The best food I tasted was the vanilla ice cream at the restaurant (The Ritzzy) in the first town. Another funny thing was when the waiter there asked if anyone wanted a spoon to taste my ice cream and he brought two giant spoons for Connie and Linda. It was fun to ride in the double-decker bus in London. Emily and I also got our first ever taxi ride there. The most unpleasant

Our crew posed for a group photo at Gatwick Airport

thing was that I forgot to bring my swimming suit. Grandpa didn't put it on the list. Aunt Connie loaned me one of her swimsuits and it fit when I pinned the straps together. The neatest thing was seeing all the sheep, lambs and cows up close. We could actually touch them," she said.

"I thought the neatest thing was getting so close to the little baby lambs," Emily said. "It was exciting to see the Wall and learn about all the things that happened there. One of the *funist* things was sitting in the upstairs front seat of the double-decker bus. We could see everything; the Queen's Guard on horseback, soldiers on parade, monuments and people shopping. The best meal was pasta at the second hotel along the Wall (Centre of Britain). We ate in a very old room with five-foot thick walls. The most unexpected thing to me was how the water tasted different here. I thought it would taste like the water does at home. I was surprised how the young people in England party. About 200 teenagers gathered in front of our hotel (Marlborough) waiting for an hour for the nightclub next door to open. They were very noisy and very badly dressed. One thing that surprised me was the five hours time difference between England and home. The most unpleasant thing about the trip was seeing the nasty boys on the beach that took all their clothes off and went swimming naked," she concluded.

"I thought the most interesting part of the trip," Linda said, "was touring Bamburgh Castle, walking through Westminster Abbey and taking the Jack the Ripper Tour. I had the most fun on the Jack the Ripper Walking Tour. The most unexpected thing about the trip was being invited to the wedding and reception at Heddon-on-the-Wall and all the questions the people there asked us. The prettiest part was the beautiful English countryside, the old buildings and magnificent rural scenery. The most unusual thing was the different old hotels we stayed at and how nice people were that I came in contact with over there. The most difficult part was the very long rides in the van, but if it weren't for that I wouldn't have seen the beautiful scenery," she said. "The ride on the underground subway was a trip in itself. I often think of the gentleman who offered me his seat. I wonder if he might have been killed on that train the next week when the bombs went off (8 July 2005 - London suicide bombers)."

"I thought the most interesting part of the trip was driving the van on the wrong side of the road," Connie said. "That was also the scariest part: driving through towns on those narrow, crooked streets with cars parked every which way along the sides of the road. The thing that surprised me most was the high cost of everything. They don't have any Dollar Stores in England. Everything costs twice as much as at home. The prettiest part was the rural countryside. Some places looked like nothing had changed for hundreds of years. The best food was the Pavlova dessert we had at the pub near Walton. The funniest part was when Allen walked off with the van key and left us stuck in Walton. Gloria, Linda and I were pretty upset at the time, but after it was over it was pretty funny. The most exciting part was getting around London on the subway and buses. The best part was getting to build wonderful memories with family," she said.

"The Wall is awesome, the people friendly and helpful, the flowers beautiful and they have a lot of cats," Gloria summarized her views of the adventure. "We encountered five beautiful cats right at the start of the walk and met more every day. I found a couple of four-leaf clovers and a six-leaf clover along the Wall path, a clear sign of good luck to come. The most unusual part was when God called **"Gloria!"** as we walked along the Wall. I couldn't imagine who in the middle of England would know my name. It turned out to be Connie calling from the van. One of the neat parts was when we found La Toot in Haltwhistle, the little variety store with the French name meaning 'this and that'. They had a lot of cat pins and cat jewelry. I really enjoyed the tour of Bamburgh Castle and especially the story of the ghost in the pink dress. I also enjoyed the quietness of the rural countryside. It was fun knitting on the Wall by Birdoswald Castle where the farmer discovered the sleeping King Arthur in the cave. London reflects the infusion of different cultures. It is more crowded and the traffic worse than when we were there before. They do have tasty food in London and interesting sights, but the city has lost some of its elegance. Harrods is not the one-of-a-kind department store it used to be. They have done away with the knitting department and we didn't see the museum-like displays of crystals, gold bath tubs and furs that made them unique," she said.

We flew out of London on July 1, 2005, exactly one week before the tragic London train bombings on July 8, 2005 that killed 56 people. Those bombings occurred in the area near our hotel. We had ridden the double-decker bus along the same route as the one that blew up. Linda and Connie had taken the same underground line on their trip to the cemetery that later blew up, and had gotten off at the station where the survivors exited. Timing is everything.

The trip has been a dream come true for me. I have made about 25 trips to England before, but usually to the cities to see the museums or churches. On this trip I wanted to see the countryside: walk where King Arthur fought his battles, sit by the quarries where the Romans dug the stones for the Wall, eat in the country pubs where farmers had enjoyed a beer and swapped tales after finishing their chores and watch the baby lambs frolicking in the fields. I haven't been disappointed. Emily, Jessica and Gloria made great walking companions, and Connie and Linda did a marvelous job driving and navigating the van. I'm ready to do it again.

Appendix A

Take to England List

Allen's Clothes

2- pair Levis
2- short sleeve shirts
2 long sleeve shirt
2 polo shirts
Sweat shirt
7-underwear
7-undershirts
2 T-shirts
wool gloves
hooded waterproof windbreaker
rain poncho
4-pair wool hiking socks
4 pair regular socks
6 hankies
walking shoes
hiking boots
swim suit
wash clothes
sun hat

Accessories

Airline tickets
Passports
Judy's approval letter
Computer
Disks

Telephone plug
Power plug adapter
Phone numbers
Address book
e-mail addresses
magnifying glass
backpack
sports bag
digital camera
camera batteries
Compass
Maps
Hadrian's Guide
Waterproof matches
First aid kit
Flashlight
Batteries
Knife
Leatherman tool
Whistle
Ziploc bags
water bottle
field glasses
Cell phones or walkie-talkies and batteries
Umbrella

Games
Uno
Cards
Paper
Markers
Books
pens

Toiletries
Overnight kit
Aspirin
Neosporin
Sunscreen
Children's aspirin
Cough medicine
Cold medicine
Alka Seltzer
10-Tide detergent

Emily's & Jessica's List
Boots
Sneakers or regular shoes
4-Wool socks
4-regular socks
7-underwear
4-short-sleeve-shirts
4-jeans or long pants
2-pair short pants
4 long-sleeve shirts
1-sweat shirts
Hooded windbreaker

Rain poncho
Sun hat
Night gown
Wool gloves
1-Beanie baby
Journal
Disposable Camera
Water bottle
Sunglasses
Whistle
Back pack
Toothbrush
umbrella

Appendix B

Where We stayed

Location	Hotel	phone
Leicester	Holiday Inn	011-44-116-249-4590
Whitley Bay	Marlborough	011-44-870-246-1825
Haltwhistle	Centre of Britain	011-44-1434-322-422
Carlisle	Angus	011-44-1228-523-546
London	St David's	011-44-207-723-3856
Gatwick	Quality Hotel	011-44-129-352-9991

Appendix C

What Did It Cost?

Hotels (for six people)

Leicester	390	
Whitley Bay	1373	
Haltwhistle	1300	
Carlisle	1843	
London	906	
Gatwick	595	$6407
Food		3,000
Van		
Hertz	1985	
Fine	153	
London parking	40	
Gas	363	2,178
Air Fares		5,984
Other Costs		
T-shirts	128	
Westminster Abby	56	
Airport parking	104	
Books	34	
Bus	40	
Phone calls	162	
Maps	75	
Guide books	100	
Misc	300	999
Total		$18,568
		$3,095 per person
		$172 per person per day

Appendix D

Things to Do and See

Aballava – at Burgh-by-Sands (milecastle 70) site of Roman fort thought to be Avalon where King Arthur was buried.

Aesica – Great Chesters (milecastle 43), Roman fort

Alnwick Castle – in Alnwick, Medieval castle

Arbeia – at South Shield — Roman fort and museum

Bamburgh Castle – north of Alnwick - 14th century castle

Birdoswald – near Gilsland – (milecastle 49) Roman fort and museum

Black Gate Museum - at Newcastle - coins and artifacts

Brocolitia – at Carrawburgh (milecastle 30) Roman fort

Broomlee Lough – (milecastle 36) treasure in lake--witches

Camboglanna – Castlesteads (milecastle 56) thought to be Camelot

Carlisle Castle – in Carlisle – Where Queen Elizabeth had her sister, Mary Queen of Scots murdered

Castle Nick – Northumberland (milecastle 39) well preserved milecastle

Cilvrnvm – Chesters (milecastle 28) Roman fort, bridge abutment and muesum

Concavata – Drumburgh (milecastle 77) Site of Roman fort

Condercvm – Benwell (milecastle 7) site of Roman Fort

Corbridge - in Corbridge (milecastle 22) Roman fort built AD 80

Coventina's Scared Well (milecastle 31) 14,000 coins found in well

Cursing Stone – in Carlisle Tullie Museum – Archbishop's curse

Durham Castle – in Durham, medieval castle

Harrow's Scar – Cumbria (milecastle 49)

Heddon-on-the Wall – (milecastle 12) Section of Hadrian's Wall

Hexham Sanctuary (milecastle 26) ancient abbey "Saxon peace stool" refuge

Legburthwaite - Castle Rock - south of Carlisle

Magnis – in Carvoran (milecastle 46) Roman fort

Maia – Bowness (milecastle 80) site of Roman fort

Mithraum – Carrawburgh (milecastle 31) temple and three altars

Museum of Antiquities – in Newcastle – Roman artifacts

North Sea – Whitley Bay Beach, nice beach

Onnvm - Halton (milecastle 21) site of Roman fort

Poltross Burn – Cumbria (milecastle 48) site of Roman fort

Pons Aelivs – Newcastle (milecastle 4)

Segedunum – Wallsend (milecastle 0) fort, museum and reconstruction

Sewingshield Crag – Sewingshields (milecastle 35) long section of Hadrian's Wall

Thirlwall Castle – in Greenhead (milecastle 46) 14th Century ruins

Vercovicium – at Housesteads (milecastle 36) fort and site museum

Vindolanda – near milecastle 39 – Roman fort from AD 85 & museum

Appendix E

Other Impressions

Emily's Hadrian's Wall journal

15 June – The flight to England was so long. I could barely sleep for an hour. I made friends with the airplane lady (flight attendant) and she would stop every time she went by to give me and Jessica a hug. She was very nice. She gave us colors and a coloring book. The dinner on the plane was good (steak) but the breakfast was not (breakfast bar). I am having so much fun here!

16 June – Grandpa got lost on the way to the hotel yesterday and again today. We saw Hadrian's Wall for the first time today. Did you know the Wall is under the streets of Newcastle? We are staying in a nice hotel by the sea.

17 June – We went back to Hadrian's Wall. Jessica, Grandpa, Grandma and I started our walk. We started close to the Wall, but then walked far from the Wall by the river. We walked more than six miles today. Grandma got tired and said a bad word. The bee sting I got on my foot the day before we left home is getting better.

18 June – We went hiking longer than yesterday. Grandma came with on the hike and she made it all the way. We saw part of Hadrian's Wall at the end of today's hike. Most of the Wall is gone. On the hike, Jessica sat down to rest and I tripped over her and fell backwards. After the hike Grandpa, Jessica and I went to the beach (the North Sea) to look for shells and rocks.

19 June – Today we walked Hadrian's Wall. It was hot. After the hike we went to a castle (Roman ruins at Corbridge) and it was beautiful. When we got home it started to rain at the hotel. The water was three-foot deep in the streets and made a waterfalls one-foot deep running down the stairs to the beach. The rain was one-foot deep on the beach.

20 June – Today we walked and it was fun, but my legs hurt. It was sunny, but it was dark in one spot because we walked through a bunch of trees close together. Aunt Connie (our support van driver) was sick today so we took a taxi to the start of our walk and walked back to our car. Grandpa told Aunt Connie and Linda (our support navigator) that he drove the van to the end and ran all the way back to start the walk with us. The hotel we are staying at is so nice.

21 June – Today I ordered a pancake at breakfast. When they brought it, it was small and really thin. They asked if I wanted another one, but I didn't know because I hadn't tasted it. Well, they brought me another one and it was big and thicker. They were good with maple syrup. We went for a hike and it was fun, but it sprinkled a little on us. Grandpa, Jessica and I walked for more than 12 miles. My feet hurt at the end of the walk.

22 June – Today we went to a museum (Roman fort) that was so cool. We got to see people dig through the ground to find things that are at least 2,000-years old. One of the diggers let us touch a piece of a post they found that was 2,000-years old. Then we went to a castle (Bamburgh Castle). It was so pretty. Did you know people still live in the castle? If I lived there I would get scared because people died there.

23 June – Today we walked about 12 miles along the Wall. Jessica and I played a trick on Grandpa. Jessica asked, "What kind of tree is that?" pointing behind Grandpa. When he turned around to look, Jessica and I ran up the hill. He stood there talking to himself. Then he turned around and saw us up the hill. We saw a baby lamb that was just a few weeks old. It was so cute. We saw two white swans in the lake and they were pretty too. Did you know we stopped and ate lunch at Robin Hood's tree? It was so neat. (The tree along Hadrian's Wall was featured in Kevin Costner's movie about Robin Hood Prince of Thieves). We went to the swimming pool after we walked today. The water was warm, but it was outdoors and the air was cold. I though it would be inside.

24 June - Today we went hiking. It was so much fun. During the hike I tricked Grandpa. He said "I'll bet you a pound we'll see part of the Wall today," and I bet him. Well we did and I gave him a pound of rocks. He meant a pound of money, which is like two of our dollars. I told him he needed to use more nouns. On the hike Jessica was eating a carrot and a baby lamb started following her because it scented the carrot. We ate dinner at the hotel we are staying at (Hotel Angus in Carlisle). The hotel is very nice. In England hotels they don't have many channels on their TV and no cartoons. Did you know England goes by a 24-hour clock?

25 June – Today we hiked and it was long. We saw blue flowers (cornflowers) that weren't forget-me-nots. They were too big for forget-me-nots. Jessica and I collected grass seeds in Jessica's hat. We collected seeds to throw in the air where Grandpa was standing. Jessica got tired of holding the hat so she put it on her head with all the seeds in her hat. She had to turn upside down to get the hat off with the seeds still in it. Then we threw the seeds on Grandpa.

26 June – Today we walked Hadrian's Wall with our English friend Hannah (we met her in Canada in 2003 during our Willmore Horseback Adventure). She knows a lot of stuff about nature. We passed a huge tree with a big hole under the roots. Then Jessica and I could just fit into the hole. It was hard going in and getting out of the hole. I stung my arm on some nettle and it blistered. Hannah gave me the leaf and I rubbed its juice on the blisters and they went back down. We saw a rare flower (orchard). It was so pretty. I found five pounds ($10) in the hotel parking lot.

27 June – Today we walked Hadrian's Wall all the way to the end. We walked for eight miles and finished two hours early. We saw lots of animals and butterflies. We didn't see the Wall today or for the last three days. There were lots of bugs flying around. I didn't find any money today but Jessica found a penny, which they call a pence here. I can't wait to get home. What is amazing is that Jessica and I got along with each other most of the time.

Jessica's Hadrian's Wall Journal

15 June – We flew on the plane for seven hours to get to England. The time here is five hours different then home (Dayton). I didn't sleep on the plane for 25 hours since I got up. I took a nap when we got to our hotel and then we went to eat. I had pasta and it was good. Emily and I have our own room in the hotel. You have to put the key card in a slot to turn on the lights. We forgot to take our key out of the slot when we went to eat and Grandpa had to get us another key.

16 June – Grandpa got lost going to our new hotel. We get lost every day. A man on a bike rode right in front of our car and Grandpa almost hit him, but we didn't. There are like no rules here about driving. They park anywhere they want and drive real fast. When we got to our hotel we had a tea party with Aunt Connie and Cousin Linda.

17 June – Today we walked more than six miles along the Wall path. We saw lots of wild flowers and dogs and five cats and a bunch of trees.

18 June – We saw lots of beautiful wild flowers today and I found a four-leaf clover. We walked up a very long hill from the river to the town where we stopped.

19 June – Today we walked Hadrian's Wall. It was much easier than yesterday's walk. We didn't find any four-leaf clovers today. We saw the Wall when we first started the walk, but not after that. When we got back to the hotel it started to rain and flooded the streets. There was thunder and lightning. It made lots of noise and music.

20 June – Today we went to walk Hadrian's Wall. I saw a tree the wind blew. The tree looked like the wind was a tornado and the tree stiffened. We got to see the Wall and it was big. When I went up to it there was a puddle of water. I stepped in it and it was muddy. I need new shoes because the mud went through to my socks. When we went to the Wall we took a taxi to the end because our driver (Connie) was sick and we walked back to the van.

21 June – We walked the Wall. This time we saw it most of the time. Today was the longest day. It is going to be the same tomorrow. We had to go up and down on hills. I was the most tired one. I dragged behind and my feet hurt the most because Emily had soccer socks on and Grandpa had wool socks on. I just had regular socks on in my hiking boots. I wear size 8 ½. I got my tooth pulled (baby molar) by Aunt Connie. She has a secret thing how she pulls it and it didn't hurt. I don't know how she did it. I got a pound (British) from the tooth fairy and that is worth two dollars.

22 June – Today we did not walk the Wall, but tomorrow we will and it will be long. We went and saw a fort. We saw a fence post 20,000-years old (2,000) and some animal bones. I felt sorry for the animals they ate, but that is life. I wanted to help find things. Then we went to a museum (Bamburgh Castle) and hear part of the story of the Pink Lady (a ghost story about a lady who jumped off the castle into the sea). I was interested in it. (Grandma bought the book). I got to hear the whole thing when we got back to the hotel. Grandma told it. After that she read us stories about dragons.

23 June – Today we walked the Wall again. I had a headache and a stomachache. We saw a baby lamb next to its mom. It was so cute. There was a dog. She was a farm dog. She followed us. She went under the fence and over the wall with barbed wire and then over the steps to stay with us. We met other people and they asked if it was our dog. We said, " No," and they said we were dognappers. I tricked Grandpa. I said,

"What is that tree?" I said to Emily, "Go." We ran and left him behind, but we waited at the top of the hill for him.

24 June – Today we hiked the Wall path, but we did not see the Wall at first. Emily asked, "Are we going to see the Wall?" "I don't know, but I'll bet you a pound that we are going to see the Wall. So later we saw the Wall. "You owe me a pound," Grandpa said to Emily. "Okay," Emily said. "Here you go," and she gave him a pound of rocks. "You need to use more nouns." When I was eating a carrot a baby lamb started to follow me so I held out my hand and said, "stay," and the lamb stopped.

25 June – Today we did not see the Wall. We were collecting seeds from a bunch of grass I was holding and a cow started following us because he wanted the grass and seeds. It was a baby cow. Then it finally stopped. We saw nine cats and a dog and lots of chickens. We saw a lot of dogs and stopped to pet them.

26 June – Today we went on the walk with Hannah who we met when we went horseback riding 16 days (Willmore Horseback Adventure). We talked about all kinds of wild flowers. We came up to a tree and the roots were out of the ground and were so huge. I climbed in it and tried to squeeze in to the roots. It was hard, but I made it. I found 10 four-leaf clovers.

27 June – Today we walked the Wall and we finished it. I am so proud that I did it. We finished early by two hours. It was amazing that Emily and I was kind to each other most of the time. My feet hurt, but I made it all the way! I found skipper's (her flat skipping rock from Whitley Bay) friends, they are rocks.

Gloria's Hadrian's Wall Journal

Nearly 2000 years after the Emperor Hadrian undertook to mark the northernmost boundary of Roman Britain with a long fortified wall, I joined Allen, Jessica and Emily along with Linda and Connie to walk the Heritage Trail along the Wall. In the mists of time I had probably heard of "Hadrian's Wall" but never gave it a second thought until Allen decided walking the Wall would an interesting escapade.

A very active and talkative Jessica sat next to me on the flight to London. When Jessica played games across with aisle with Emily, I read the latest Lillian Jackson Braun cat mystery. The book lasted the entire trip. Collecting our luggage and getting onto the carts provided turned out to be no easy task. The wheels on my cart were askew. Consequently, the thing had a tendency to go in circles. I got caught in the middle of the street with the circle dance. Fortunately, Connie saw what was happening and came to my rescue before I encountered any traffic complications.

Thursday, June 16, we headed for Newcastle where the Wall began. The Heritage Museum is equipped with all the history, trials and tribulations you need to know to make the trip as interesting as possible. There are artifacts, dioramas, paintings, and all kinds of games and activities to inform you of how the area appeared when the Wall was built and life thrived along it. The gift shop provided the opportunity to purchase a Hadrian's Wall passport so that it could be stamped at different stops along the way and plenty of souvenir merchandise, cards and books were available.

The starting point, the Segedunum, is still being excavated, but a sampling of the Wall helped us to see how the original looked and prepared us for what to expect in the way of scenery, excavations, forts, etc. along the way.

Parts of the original Wall remain standing; other sections have been plundered for houses, highways, roads and fences. Some of it still is hidden underground and is being excavated – forts, milecastles, towers, other structures and artifacts are being discovered every day. It is a dynamic process that is going to take years to complete.

Interest in this adventure expanded as I realized that this walk was going to start at the North Sea and proceed to the Irish Sea. Intrigue entered with the knowledge that King Arthur and Camelot at one time flourished along part of the wall. I discovered a diverse range of unforgettable scenery, a vast range of ancient and modern attractions stretching from east coast to west coast along with some of the friendliest and most interesting people one could meet anywhere in the world. The trek from coast to coast along the Heritage Trail promised a wide range of ancient and modern attractions as well as challenges.

I knew from the beginning that there would be days I couldn't walk the trail for one reason or another. First of all, the medication I take for high blood pressure. Prolonged direct sunlight is taboo. Also, toward the end of the walk the trail became much too challenging for the amount of training I had done, but shopping would compensate for those times as well as having knitting time in the van.

Knitting needles are still forbidden items on some flights and I didn't want to take the chance of having any of my equipment confiscated. I read books on the flights to and from and took out my knitting gear for the days that were to be spent in the van with Connie and Linda. I selected Debbie New's Dish Cloth vest from *Unexpected Knitting* to be worked on. It is an easy piece done in sections to be joined later. It turned out to be good travel knitting during the van time and in the evenings in the hotels. Pieces are complete and assembly is required. At one point Allen took a picture of me sitting on the Wall knitting, the section where the serf dropped his clew of yarn and found the entryway to King Arthur's tomb. The entrance possibly could be there sealed deep in the earth.

On Friday, June 17th, the trek started. Five beautiful feral cats saw us off. There was marmalade striped one; another black and white job watched us carefully as we walked by. A small gray tabby looked at us as if to say, "Are you going to eat me?" The others eyed us with apprehension. We moved along and they did too.

That first day of the walk inspired us. There were yellow, pink, blue flowers of all sorts growing profusely along the bike path. Huge four-leaf clovers crowded the edge of the path and I found a 6-leaf clover, 4 leaves surrounding 2 stand-up leaves in the center. Over hill and dale we hiked along the bike path. Traffic crossings interrupted the trail ever so often. Emily and Jessica rescued night crawlers when they came upon them and played with roly-poly along the way. It was a leisurely walk so that nothing of interest could be missed.

An acorn symbol as well as frequent signs marked the trail along the bike path, through crowded city streets, following the river wending our way to the area where Connie and Linda would pick us up. Happiness with the trail and surroundings wore quite thin as we trudged along crowded city streets, dragged along through industrial areas and struggled with careless, rude bikers speeding along the pedestrian areas.

Dinner that evening at a family restaurant salvaged the day. The owner and his son recommended their specialties. Emily and I shared a large, medium well-cooked steak smothered in mushrooms, accompanied by crispy onion rings and French fries. I selected a lemon blue for dessert from the owner's special tray. The large slice of cheese cake dribbled with heavy, sweat cream and contained blueberries. It made the taste buds quiver and felt like velvet to the stomach.

Saturday, June 18th, second day of the walk appeared to be fairly flat and my kind of terrain for walking. The sun came and went, but the air was still cool. Circumstances deteriorated as I progressed along the trail. By this time I had found out that there a British Mile is different from a U. S. mile in length. No one told me the exact difference, but the British mile is longer. What was supposed to be a six-mile walk turned into a little over eight-miles and I was painin' and achin' by the time I climbed the cobblestone 400 foot high incline to the top where the van would be waiting still a mile farther on. The cow path high above the river turned out to be treacherous and difficult walking. Then there was the section along the farmer's wheat field that proved to be a prickly experience.

Numerous small adventures befell us along the trail on this day. Met a nice gentleman and his dog Sasha. Sasha's owner provided quite a bit of detailed information as to what we could expect as we walked the Wall. He lived in the area and had hike the entire Wall at one time, plus still walking along a section or so each day.

While we were visiting with Sasha and his owner, taking pictures and enjoying being out in the country far away and across an ocean from anyone I knew, a voice called out, "Gloria!" I thought I must be dreaming until it came again, "GLORIA!"

Was it God calling out to me? Who could possibly call me by my first name this far away from home and in the middle of northern England? I turned the direction of the call and there down on the regular road was our van and Connie was hollering out the window. "We're lost!" she said.

She and Linda had missed our bridge rendezvous point and were driving around in circles. A meeting point at a definite pub was established and we were on our way again.

So far we had walked along the bikeway, the river, through cow pastures, wheat fields, city streets, through industrial areas and now we were going to cross a golf course. Yes, there were golfers out there, but we made it across none the worse for wear. Until… at the end, Jessica sat down to tie her shoe and Emily fell over her.

Earlier we had lunch at The Boathouse, a pub recommended by our friend earlier on the trail. Only hamburger pie (a shepherd's pie) was available because the cook was getting married that day and only the bar maid was on duty. This is a tasty dish with hamburger and mixed vegetables and meat juice topped by mashed potatoes.

Leaving the pub and continuing along the trail, we came upon a park with an ice cream wagon. A young man took a picture of the four of us.

We at supper that evening at a British fast food place located at the Open Market – chaos of traffic and people. Emily and I shared a cheeseburger platter and then dashed out to shop in the open market for gifts and fudge. I bought some rum truffle fudge. This capped the longest walk I've done in years plus the fact the sun was bearing down on me at the end of the cobblestone climb struggling along all the twists, turns and uphill grades of assorted housing areas. The next few days I spent in the van out of the sun and knitting.

Sunday, June l9th, Fathers Day dawned bright, sunny and hot. We found lunch at The Robin Hood's tavern and it was terrific. It consisted of a well done pork roast with assorted veggies. Linda, Connie and I had been allowed to sit in the area before lunch so that I could knit and we could wait until the others arrived. The décor was rustic logs and plaster, old world atmosphere and friendly people.

This was our last night at the Marlborough Hotel. Sunday in England finds all shops and stores closed tightly. The only place to buy any food or necessities after the noon dinner hours are over are petrol stations. We got in line for chips and ice cream and watched the sky as storm clouds gathered. Following those storm clouds to our hotel, we discovered the street to our hotel blocked off. Barricades and flashing red and plus police car lots barred passage. Allen took some back streets until we could double back to our hotel. The sea front area was totally flooded and water was gurgling in the streets. Lots of people gathered to stand at the bridge and look down at the boiling, bubbling ocean. Turned out it was the worst storm in the area in 20 years.

Monday, 20 June – coming into The Centre of Britain. Connie couldn't drive because she had an upset stomach, her back hurt, and stress of traffic had taken its toll on her nerves. Allen took her to a surgery (doctor's office) and pills were prescribed as well as a trip to the chemist's (drug store).

We had to wait for our rooms, but the hotel management got Connie and Linda into their unit right away. Three separate bi-level units had been reserved for us located at the rear of the main building and away from the main street, basically our own private place. The stay here would be four days. Wonderful! Dinner was served in our own formal dining room.

21 June – This is the longest day of the year and it's raining. A strenuous 10-mile walk is ahead for Allen, Jessica and Emily. Connie feels better with the pills and relief of driving duties. She is doing the laundry. Connie, Linda and I had lunch at the Manor House Pub across the street from the hotel. Rain stopped about mid-morning and a nice breeze took over. The prawn salad I had for lunch made my day. Lots of tasty pink prawns crowded on a bed of lettuce with tomatoes on the side.

Knitting is going well. Started my first turquoise module for the vest. The other module is a jewel toned variegate color. The vest is progressing and the colors are striking.

Shopped at La Toot (French word for this and that) this morning. Lots of cat items in stock. Connie bought some for gifts as did Linda and I. The lady made iced tea for Linda which is quite an event. The British do not drink iced tea. She made tea and then poured it over glass of ice cubes. Turned out to be a nice cool day with misty rain. Allen and girls walked 12 tough miles along the wall. Dinner at the manor house consisted of vegetable la sagna for me. There were an awful lot of small green peas. The French fries are good, quite different from ours, more like our fried potatoes. The ever-present salad of lettuce and tomatoes set off the meal.

Connie is recovering from her misadventure and Linda is doing well with her cast.

June 22 — This is a day off from walking and Allen has planned for us to tour Bamburg Castle. The spectacular scenery along the way – flowers, greenery, hills and dales, blue skies and sunshine really paved the way for this castle high on a hill. After parking the car, the climb to the entrance was long and winding up a stone trail. Looking to the left we were right alongside the blue ocean, high up the hill from the surface.

The gentleman who welcomed us at the door turned out to be a cheery and informative fellow. Immediately to the left of the entrance stood a chain-mail exhibit. Now was the time to find out if the stories of knitting chain-mail were true. The very heavy chain-mail had to be made by blacksmiths with special training. Small chain mail was crafted from special pieces as it got lighter. He did say that some of it may have been knitted while the knitters were watching the executions.

Lances, spears, armor clothing and shoes of medieval times filled many of the rooms. A Bamburg dragon existed as a coat of arms and the castle has a ghost – the Pink Lady.

It wouldn't be a medieval castle without a ghost; Bamburgh Castle with a bright blue sky above us, a swirling sea around huge crags from which the traditional fairy-tale turrets and battlements rise, can cast a spell that reaches back into the mists of time. There is a female phantom in a pink dress which haunts this castle. Story has it that her father disapproved of the boy she was in love with and sent the unfortunate suitor overseas for seven years. He forbid the couple to exchange messages and hoped that his daughter's passion would cool. The young woman became more and more depressed.

In a final attempt to persuade his daughter to give up her love, the king told her that his spies had discovered that the boy had married someone else abroad. However, to cheer her up after this devastating news, the king asked the castle seamstress to make a fine dress in his her favorite color – pink. The distraught girl donned the finished garment, climbed the stairway to the highest battlements, and flung herself to her death on the rocks below. Shortly afterwards her lover returned from his exile, unmarried, and was heartbroken by what had happened.

Every seven years the princess clothed in a dress of shimmering pink, wanders through the corridors of the oldest section of the castle before gliding down the rocky path that leads to the beach. Here she stands upon the sands, gazing sadly out to sea, forever awaiting the return of her lost love. Rumor has it that this she can be seen at this time by visitors to the castle.

I found a book of dragon stories in the castle gift shop. At the rate of one dragon story a night the book provided entertainment for Jessica and Emily during the rest of the trip. Clever little stories which they enjoyed.

June 23 – Connie was back in shape again and could drive along the winding country, scenic roads. Visited archeological digs – touched a 2000 year-old fence post remains – climbed up and stood on part of Hadrian's Wall.

Friday – June 24: We left Haltwhistle and drove to a Roman fort to start Allen and the girls off on the day's trek. Misty rain in the early morning refreshed everyone, but the sun came up and turned on the heat. We shopped, found a tea shop where we stopped for lunch.

Vickie's Hill – driving by pony farm – overshot our destination to Roman fort and actually went half-way to Walton, the end of the trek for the day. Allen's directions proved to have some flaws. He gave us a couple of right turns that should have been lefts. When we hit the three-pronged fork, we took a wrong turn the first time. Discovered our mistake and doubled back.

Scenery and flowers along the road prolific and spectacular. Working on Dish Cloth Vest each night. Starting Module #5. Colors are blending together well.

Allen took my picture sitting on Hadrian's Wall knitting at the point where the serf dropped his clew down the yawning hole and found King Arthur and company. He blew it all by forgetting to blow the horn.

Getting into Carlisle and locating our Angus hotel at rush hour proved to be challenging. Everyone was stressed out. Connie panicked about driving in the city, Jessica and Emily were exhausted and emotional.

Supper was grand – I had a glass of Liebermilch and a delicious salmon sautéed in white wine sauce and smothered in prawns. Cheesy mashed potatoes accompanied the salmon along with an array of fresh vegetables – broccoli, navy beans and cauliflower, carrots and the ever-present zucchini.

For dessert apple flan with cream which was a shock because instead of a crumbly biscuit, sugared crust with apples and whipped cream – no cream poured over it as we had grown accustomed to on former trips to England. Good, but not what was expected.

Connie and Linda traded rooms with Jessica and Emily. The room Jessica and Emily had at first was quite a bit larger than the one next to us. Our room is nice – bedroom, desk room plus a large bathroom

Early morning walk with Allen – bright blue star flowers, white daisies, purple bells, gardens are eye candy of color and an assortment of plants. Calm walk because traffic hasn't picked up for rush hour.

Girls found a blue plastic star on trail. Landscape is dotted with sheep which outnumber cows and horses – roads twist and turn and are hardly wide enough for two cars, sometimes only one. People park on sidewalks. They drive fast, but have good manners still prevail, saw bunnies and pheasant along road – one hare which is a large bunny. No wool shops sighted, but rumors were that they existed in the larger towns.

Hadrian's Wall is impressive – but I wanna go home. Three more nights here and 3 in London – get to visit Stan on Thursday – then we are homeward bound. I miss Mai-Tai.

This is Saturday, June 25 For supper Jessica had chicken pieces shaped like teddy bears. Day had a rough start – Allen forgot to leave the keys to the van when he and the girls took off on the day's trek. We tried to reach him by radio – nothing. What are we to do? We can't leave the van. Would we be here until 4 o'clock or later. I actually started down the trail after them, but soon realized they were too far ahead for me to catch them. Connie and I were rippin' and rarin'. Linda was whining. No one came by on the trail. I refused to put up with any more bellyaching. Lady came by with dog. She listened to the tale of our plight and said she would drive us all to Carlisle to the hotel. Connie and I decided she could take Linda back and we would stay with the van for however long it took. Maybe if we went to one of the crossroads and met them –

We prayed, whined and cussed. I kept trying the radio – stone silence. Lord, please let him realize the keys are in his pocked. I knitted, Connie crocheted and Linda got out of van to look at the flowers growing around. A half hour more passed and the lady came up the lane in her car.

Connie yells out, "Thank God – here he comes!" Allen came jogging down the lane. Connie ran to meet him. "This was a test," he said. "I bet you were cussin'.

"You're right. We did it all – moaning, groaning, cussing, praying, knitting and crocheting. Your ears must have been burning."

We were walking along making pretty good time. Started up a hill and I felt the keys in my jeans pocket. Nearly to the crossroad. Jessica and Emily started entertaining themselves gathering reeds and awaiting Grandpa's return. Met our benefactor. We all felt much better. Allen got in the car to drive to the crossroad. What a way to start the day.

We couldn't use the radio. It was deader than a doornail without the car running. We hadn't realized how far up the creek without a paddle we were. We waited at the crossing as Allen went back to the girls. He was to radio us when they connected. He did.

Connie wanted to stay at the crossing until it was time when she could call Tracy. Meanwhile the little girls came around the turn with Allen. They had a bag full of seeds they had collected to throw at him along the trail.

At last the walkers were under way and our radio was working. Connie made her call and it was lunch time – Salutation Pub — Chocolate Pavlova dessert – lacy chocolate wall over meringue base – cylinders of meringue around chocolate ice cream with a dab of unsweetened whipped cream on the top – spikey bowl filled with meringue and chocolate ice cream. A dream of dessert come true. We savored it.

Tea rejuvenated us – the soup proved to be edible – carrot and carob – kind of a sweet soup with a herbal bite to it. Didn't really care for it.

Returned to the hotel with ease because we missed the rush and buzz of heavy traffic. Jessica chided Allen along the trail because of the essence of cow poop – he had sat on a cow patty to rest. The Lord had turned what appeared to be a bad day at first into a fine adventure foodwise and scenery wise.

Hannah, a wrangler from the Mount Willmore horseback trip, is schedule to come to our hotel tonight. There is a room reserved for her.

Connie is enjoying the trip at this point because with Hannah's visit she won't have to drive for the next two days. A cab will be used to get from point to point to pick up the car. Traffic is much too congested and stressful to drive. Two more days and the walk is over.

Jessica and Emily are real troopers, eating well and walking strong. Jessica eats a lot of veggies and is talking about going vegetarian. They are getting along well, lots of energy and enjoying their nightly dragon story.

Hannah is a vibrant and terrific person to talk to, a very small woman, and looks like a teenage.
She walked Sunday with girls and Allen. Girls got into nettles, quite painful, sticky plant. Hannah pulled off a healing leaf from a nearby plant. It worked wonders.

Allen found Camelot yesterday after the finished the Wall walk. Connie got out of the car and followed his trail through the woods to a footbridge. A house is built on the Camelot site, but the setting is lovely. King Arthur was born in Tintagel, fought at this fort and along the Wall (Camelot) and is buried at Avalon.

Weather has been nice and cool up until Sunday, clouds were fluffy. Now the temps have gone up. Have seen a cat or so here and there.

28 June – We finished the Wall walk, had our Wall passports stamped at each station along the way. Allen bought T-shirts for all of us with a map of the Wall on the back, "I Walked the Wall" on the front.

Conclusions: The Wall is awesome, people are friendly and helpful, lots of assorted cats and beautiful flowers, and the scenery is amazing. London reflects the infusion of different cultures and is more crowded, traffic is heavier. The food is tasty and always interesting. There is a strong trend to spices. Dishcloth vest is almost complete except for assembling.

Carlisle Castle is where Queen Elizabeth had her sister Mary Queen of Scots murdered.

London has lost a lot of its elegance and eloquence. Harrods is dreadful, just another department store, not the one-of-a-kind store as in the past. No more knitting department. Easy to get lost in. Some of the employees cannot even find the restrooms.

Trip back to Gatwick motel a nightmare of traffic and roads, but the motel itself comfortable, served great food and a mighty breakfast. Flight home on time and restful.

Rain fell, mist seeped around us on occasion, and the sun shone a lot. Walking the Wall is a terrific adventure through scenery, meeting nice people, interesting sights such as the eye-lid bridge, fascinating people who work in the pubs. A super experience on all levels: sights to see, refreshing rain to feel, cats soft fur to touch, smelling the many varied flowers, and listening to the varied sounds of the cities as well as the quietness of the countryside.

Food is a culinary experience and adventure from the chocolate Pavlova to the teddy bear chicken strips. Allen ordered crepes and ice cream on one occasion. The waitress served with a flick of the wrist and dumped the ice cream in Linda's lap before the crepes reached Allen. Waitress replaced the order while we cleaned Linda up.

The Wall dominated our conversation because of the ancient forts and excavation we toured as well as the ups and down of the entire trail which wound its way through city street, industrial areas, along biked paths, through farmers' fields and pastures. We met people from several different nations who were friends and took time to chat with us.

The hotels we stayed in were varied and comfortable. People who operated them took pride in their establishments and catered to the wants and needs of their guests. Many were family owned and operated.

Connie's and Linda's Walk With Jack The Ripper

One of the highlights of the trip to England for Connie and Linda turned out to be the night in London when they decided to walk the dark side of London on a Jack the Ripper tour. (www.jack-the-ripper-tour.net Cost £5. Tour starts every night at the exit of the **Tower Hill Underground** station at 6:45 p.m., no need to book. Phone 020-7480-6453.)

Jack the Ripper is a name that instantly conjures up images of gas lights and creeping fog, wet cobblestone streets and an unseen killer stalking those streets. For a little over two chilling hours Linda and Connie joined a small group of other interested thrill-seekers delving into the crooked alleyways of Whitechapel to follow the Ripper's bloodstained trail of terror. They took the underground train from Paddington Station to Tower Hill Station to follow the trail of terror step-by-step.

To get into the mood and atmosphere of autumn 1888 they participated in a short orientation session which included an account of the major events that surrounded the Whitechapel murders. By becoming familiar with the facts of the Jack the Ripper history, they could ask questions and better understand how every piece of the puzzle fit into place. The names of the police officers involved were listed as well as pictures of the unfortunate victims.

Jack the Ripper was not the world's first serial killer, but he was the first media murderer. When his crimes took place, literacy among the general population was increasing. The press at large became a catalyst for social change. Articles about the murders appeared in the newspapers on a daily basis and fostered a general fascination that at times bordered on hysteria. Press coverage helped turn the crimes into a phenomenon and transformed a sordid back street killer into an international legend. Within ten weeks he struck five times. His victims were the women who would give themselves to anyone who would pay them the price of a glass of gin. The killer was never caught and has been the subject of speculation and controversy ever since. To this day he is known at "Jack the Ripper."

Connie and Linda along with other members of the tour were transported back to that long ago era on a journey through the very streets where the infamous Whitechapel murders occurred. Through the guide's storytelling they joined the Victorian police as they raced against time to stop Jack the Ripper before he could kill again. They also explained the reasons why they found it so difficult to hunt him down.

The nocturnal journey continued through back alleyways where they had the opportunity to see original documents and actual police photographs of the crime scenes and even the poor victims themselves. They could sift through evidence to eliminate suspect after suspect and hear the most up to date theories concerning the killer's true identity. Their experience was enhanced with historic photographs of the streets through which they passed and the sites on which they stood as the streets were in 1888 to get the full atmosphere of the area.

The first murder victim, Mary Ann Nichols, was a 43-year-old prostitute who had been evicted from her lodging house two hours earlier because she had no money to pay her rent. Her throat had been cut.

The second victim, Annie Chapman, was discovered in John Davis's backyard at 29 Hanbury Street. Her body was mutilated and a few feet away lay a folded, wet leather apron. Since the leather apron was the standard garment worn by a wide range of Jewish workers from butchers to tailors, the finding of such a garment caused the neighborhood to erupt into anti-Semitism.

The Whitechapel murders continued with Elizabeth Stride and her throat had been slashed. The Ripper came close to being caught at this one. Since there were no mutilations to the body, the police concluded that the murderer had been interrupted as he went about his bloody business. Is it possible that, as he stooped over his victim, the noise of the cheap jewelry hawker's cart entering the area had disturbed him, causing him to move back quickly into the shadows? Perhaps it was this sudden movement that had startled the pony?

The informative Jack the Ripper walk continued to the night of September 30, 1888, the night of the double murder. This is the night when the police came closest to catching the ripper and the night when Jack left his only clue behind.

At around 8:30 AM the previous evening Officer Louis Robinson of the City Police had arrested 46-year-old Catharine Eddowes on Aldgate High Street and charged her with being drunk and disorderly. She was taken to Bishopsgate police station, placed in a cell and left to sober up. As Elizabeth Stride was meeting her murderer, Catherine was heard singing and was deemed sober enough for immediate release. Leaving the station around 1 AM she turned to the desk sergeant and spoke her last recorded words, "Cheerio me old cock," she called and stepped out into the early morning. At approximately 1:35 AM three men were leaving the imperial club at 16-17 Duke Street. They noticed a man and a woman talking with one another at the corner of Church Passage. One of the three would later give the police a detailed description of this mystery man and maintain that the woman whom he saw was definitely Catharine Eddowes.

In the aftermath of the "Double Event" police activity intensified throughout early October. Extra police patrolled the streets. Despite lurid rumors and several scares the intensification of police activity appeared to have deterred the Ripper and October passed with no further murders.

Mary Jane Kelly, 25 years old, became the Ripper's last victim. This one was the goriest of all. On the 9th of November, George Hutchinson, encountered Mary Kelly on Commercial Street. She cheerfully asked him for sixpence, to which he replied that even this amount was beyond his means. She laughed and told him she'd "just have to find it some other way" and continued to the junction with Thrawl Street where she met another man. Hutchinson saw the two chat a bit, then watched as Mary led the man into Dorset Street where they entered her room in Miller's Court. Forty-five minutes later neither had emerged from the room and Hutchinson left the scene.

Shortly before 4 AM several of Mary's neighbors were roused by a cry of "*Murder*," but all chose to ignore it.

At 10:45AM when Thomas Bowyer called to collect her overdue rent he discovered her mutilated body. The murderer had left the room in Miller's Court and disappeared into the early morning. With no one gazing upon the body of poor, unfortunate Mary Kelly could have realized was that in that blood-bath of Miller's Court, the Ripper's reign of terror would end as suddenly and mysteriously as it had begun. As he left the bloody scene in that small room that morning, the Whitechapel Murderer may have performed his swan song, but the legend of Jack the Ripper was only beginning.

Connie and Linda both enjoyed the tour immensely and felt it definitely had been informative and well worth the time and money spent.

Appendix F

British – American Dictionary

British	**American**
Angry	mad
Articulated lorry	tractor trailer
Banger	sausage
Bap	hamburger bun
Bathing costume	bathing suit
Biscuit	cookie
Blind summit	limited visibility
Bollards	traffic cones dividing highway
Bonnet (car)	hood
Boot (car)	trunk
Braces	suspenders
Bum	butt
Burn	small stream
Candy floss	cotton candy
Canteen	cafeteria
Car park	parking lot
Caravan	trailer or RV
Chemist	pharmacist
Chips	french fries
Cinema	movie house
Clingfilm	saran wrap
Courgette	zucchini
Crag	steep, rugged rock cliff
Crisp	potato chips
Dene	valley

220

Dummy tit	pacifier
Dustbin	garbage can
Earth rod	electrical ground
Elastoplast	Band Aid
Estate agent	realtor
Face flannel	wash cloth
Fell	hillside
Film	movie
Firth	water passage where tide meets river.
Flitting	moving your residence without paying the rent
Flat	apartment
Football	soccer
Fortnight	two weeks
Garage	gas station
Garden	yard
Give way	yield
Gorse	juniper bush
Ground floor	first floor
Half seven (time)	seven thirty
Headmaster	principal
Holiday	vacation
Hoover	vacuum cleaner
Ill	sick
Industrial estate	business park
Jacket potato	baked potato
Jam	jelly
Jelly	Jell-O
Jumper	sweater
Keep your pecker up	keep your chin up

Knickers	ladies underwear
Knock you up	wake you up
Ladyfinger	okra
Lead	leash (dog)
Lemonade	Sprite or 7-Up
Lift	elevator
Lolly	sucker
Loo	toilet
Lorry	truck
Lounge	living room
Mackintosh	raincoat
Mad	crazy
Minced beef	ground beef
Moor	boggy area of wasteland
Moulting	shedding
Nappy	diaper
Parcel	package
Pavement	sidewalk
Peckish	hungry
Perambulator	baby carriage
Petrol	gasoline
Porridge	oatmeal
Postal code	zip code
Postman	mailman
Power point	electrical outlet
Pub	bar
Queue	line
Redundant (to be made)	laid off
Ring (telephone)	call
Roundabout	rotary
Rubber	eraser

Rubbish	trash
Rucksack	backpack
Sacked	fired
Sanitary towel	sanitary napkin
Sellotape	scotch tape
Serviette	napkin
Shop	store
Sideboards	sideburns
Silencer	muffler
Single ticket	one way ticket
Sitting in a tailback	stuck in a traffic jam
Sleeping policeman	speed bump
Smalls	underwear
Solicitor	lawyer
Spanner	wrench
Sultanas	seedless raisins
Surgery	doctor's office
Tap	faucet
Tarn	small, steep-banked mountain lake.
Taxi	cab
Tights	pantyhose
Tin	can
Toilet	restroom
Tomato sauce	catsup
Torch	flashlight
Trainers	sneakers
Treacle	molasses
Trolley	shopping cart
Trousers	pants
Unadopted street	private street

Underground	subway
Verge	shoulder (road)
Vest	undershirt
Vicus	people living next to Roman fort who provided labor.
Waist coat	vest
Wardrobe	closet
White sauce	white gravy with cheese
Wold	elevated track of uncultivated land.

References

Bamburgh Castle, Jarrold Publishing, Norwich, England, 2001

Birley, Anthony R., Hadrian, The Restless Emperor; Routledge, London, 1997.

Birley, Robin C., Roman Records From Vindolanda, Roman Amy Museum Publications, Carvoran, England, 1999

Birley, Robin C., Vindolanda, Roman Army Museum Publications, Carvoran, England 2004

Breeze, David J., Hadrian's Wall, English Heritage, London, England, 2003

Burton, Anthony, Hadrian's Wall Path, Aurum Press, London, England, 2003

Cabasin, Linda, editor, Fodor's, Fodor's Travel Publications, NY, NY 2004

Cox, Phil Roxbee, Who Were the Romans?, English Heritage, London, England, 2002

Crow, James, Housesteads, A Fort and Garrison on Hadrian's Wall, Tempus Publishing, Stroud, England, 2004

Divine, David, Hadrian's Wall, A Study of the North West Frontier of Rome; Gambit Inc, Boston MA, 1969.

Dore, J.N., Corbridge Roman Site, English Heritage, London, England, 2001

Griffiths, W.B., Segedunum, Roman Fort, Bath and Museum, Tyne and Wear Museum, Newcastle England, 2001

Harrison, David, Along Hadrian's Wall; Cassell & Company, London, 1956.

Hebbert, Antonia, editor, Secret Britain, Automobile Association, Fanum House, Basingstoke, Hampshire, UK, 1986

Henderson, Joan, The Laidley Worm of Bamborough, Newcastle upon Tyne City Libraries & Arts, Newcastle England, 1991.

Johnson, Paul, Castles of England, Scotland and Wales, Weidenfeld and Nicolson Ltd, London, UK, 1989.

Johnson, J.S., Chesters Roman Fort, English Heritage, London, England, 2004

Pitkin, King Arthur, Jarrold Publishing, Norwich, England, 2005

<u>Roman Britain</u>, Historical Map and Guide: Ordnance Survey, Southhampton UK, 5th edition.

Stone, Lucy, editor, <u>Exploring Britain</u>, Jarrold Publishing, Norwich, UK, 1991

Index

Order Form for Allen's Books

[ ] Walking Hadrian's Wall

"This part of the Wall is 2,000-years old," I told my wife and 12-year-old twin granddaughters as we stood by a section of Hadrian's Wall in Newcastle, England. We had come to walk the 80-mile long wall that the Emperor of Rome built in AD 120 to protect Roman settlements in Southern England from the Barbarians in the north.

The Wall has mostly disappeared at both ends where people borrowed the stones to build churches, barns, houses and farm walls. We followed the path along where the Wall used to be and occasionally caught a glimpse of the actual remains of the 10-foot thick, 15-foot high limestone wall Hadrian built.

The middle section of the Wall is nearly all intact as it passes through the sparsely-populated Lake District. We stopped to explore the remains of the milecastles, watchtowers and bridges, and took side trips to view the excavations of the nearby Roman forts. The granddaughters kept up a brisk pace as we climbed up and down 400-foot high hills following the Wall over steep, craggy cliffs and beside picturesque lakes filled with ducks and wild swans. Passing a quaint white stone cottage set back in the woods, our granddaughters encountered nine cats and stopped to pet them.

After 10 days of hiking, we arrived at Bowness-on-Solway by the Irish Sea and found the wooden shelter that marked the end of the walk. Emily and Jessica clasped their hands over my head as we took the obligatory end-of-walk photo to prove we completed the entire 100-mile-long path along Hadrian's Wall.

"I'm so proud that I finished the whole walk," granddaughter Jessica said. "I'm going to have my shoes bronzed!"

ISBN 1-880675-09-9   **$15.00**

[ ]   Willmore Horseback Adventure

A 500-pound grizzly bear chased a ground squirrel a scant 100 feet from us while her twin cubs watched. Emily and Jessica sat quiet as church mice as the chase continues. With a flying leap, the sow bear caught the squirrel and fed it to her hungry cubs.

My 9-year-old twin granddaughters, Emily and Jessica, joined four hikers seven wranglers and me on 16-day horseback adventure in the Canadian Rocky Mountains of Alberta Canada. The Wild Rose Outfitters used 24 pack horsed and 10 riding horses to take us deep into the 1,700 square mile wilderness park without roads, bridges, houses or permanent residents.

We camped at six remote sites high in the Rocky Mountains. A sugar-coating of frost covered our tents each morning. During the day, we rode over snow-covered mountain passes, through virgin spruce forests, across rain-swollen rivers and along knife-edge ridges to see some of the most spectacular wilderness country in the world.

Our cook prepared gourmet meals in a wilderness camp environment: charcoal-grilled steak, pork chops, lasagna, shepard's pie and salmon with a different type of fresh salad every night and our choice of red and white wine for supper.

When Emily and Jessica weren't on the trail they were wading in the creek, chasing butterflies, shooting at tin cans with their slingshots, fishing, roasting marshmallows, reading stories, making dream catchers, looking for fossils or begging Dave to play the "Pickle" song on his guitar so they could sing along.

The horseback ride turned out to be the adventure of a lifetime.

ISBN 1-880675-08-0   **$15.00**

[ ]   Kayaking Around Iceland

Emily and Jessica, the author's 8-year-old granddaughters, embarked on a kayaking trip in the Arctic Ocean around Iceland with the author and a friend. One of the days, the sunny, windless, glassy-smooth fjord turn into a gray, foamy torrent of wind-whipped white-capped waves in less than an hour. Paddling back to the mainland became an exciting adventure. The other days of kayaking turned out to be much more mundane. They experienced beautiful sunny, calm weather, picturesque green fjords, sparkling waterfalls, colorful puffin birds and snow-covered mountains in the background.

Besides kayaking, they visited waterfalls, geysers, glaciers, bird cliffs, geothermal pools and gorgeous black-sand beaches. Emily counted 1,004 waterfalls while they drove 2,000 miles through the Iceland countryside. One windy day they visited the Latrabjarg bird cliffs where millions of puffins, kittiwakes, gulls, and cormorants nest.

ISBN 1-880675-07-2   **$15.00**

[ ]   Sweden through the Eyes of a
Six-Year-old

Trolls, fairies, kings, butterflies, hedgehogs and relatives:
that's what my granddaughter experienced on our bicycle ride
through Sweden. Six-year-old Emily and Jessica biked 400
miles across rural Sweden on a tag-along attached to the seat
of my bicycle. "You can't go too fast, Grandpa or we'll miss
something," they told me. So we rode a moderate speed and
stopped every 20 or 30 minutes so the girls could chase
butterflies, eat wild strawberries, run up the hill, pick
wildflowers or take a nap.

We bike over the Gota Canal, swam in the crystal-clear Baltic
Sea, slept at a spa dating back to the 1700s, explored the 800-
year-old fortress walls of Visby, visited 13th century churches
and ate smoked eel. As we rode through enchanted forest we
kept our eyes peeled for trolls and while we didn't actually see
them we could hear and smell them—they smell like fresh turned
earth.

We saw spectacular rural scenery, the sparkling Baltic Sea,
deer, hedgehogs, fox, rabbits, hares, wild peacock, eagles,
Gotland ponies, butterflies and more red Swedish barns than I
could imagine. My 6-year-old granddaughters impressed my
by pedaling for 6 to 8 hours a day for 11 days and still maintained
a positive, upbeat, inquisitive attitude.

ISBN 1-880675-06-4   **$15.00**

237

[ ] ROLLERBLADING ACROSS HOLLAND

In the summer of 1998, Allen, Kelsey (11-years old) and Karla Reichert, a family friend, rollerbladed 365 miles around Holland carrying a backpack. They started in Amsterdam, skated to the coast of the North Sea, followed the coastline down to Belgium, skated in to Antwerp and back up to Amsterdam. They encountered windmills, dikes, polders, dams, canals, monasteries, medieval churches, a diamond factory, castles and beaches.

The trio averaged 25-miles per day by skating 5 to 7 hours. They stopped often to explore windmills, swim in the North Sea, tour the unique storm surge barriers that keeps the sea out of the Dutch lowlands, visit with the local people and see the local sights.

The food in Holland and Belgium was both delicious and attractively presented. They dined on lobster salads, chicken breast covered with nuts, Argentine steaks, Chinese and Japanese delicacies, a dozen kinds of pasta, and dozens of different cheeses.

The trio agreed rollerbladed swam in the North Sea 10 times, ate 103 scoops of delicious Dutch ice cream, sampled 38 different kinds of cheese and attended a flower auction where 17-million flowers are sold each day. I'd call that a successful trip!

ISBN 1-880675-04-8   **$15.00**

[ ]   BIKING TO THE ARCTIC CIRCLE

"Bike to the Arctic Circle? Impossible! There's ice and snow up there," my friend said. Regardless, I did cycle to the Arctic Circle.

As a child I dreamed of traveling the Alaskan Highway. When I started planning the trip our grandson agreed to bike the 1,000 mile Alaskan Highway portion. My office-mate rode the first 800 miles, our niece cycled across Canada and my neighbor rode the Alaskan portion.

The prettiest part of our lower-48-state ride was biking along the Mississippi River's Great River Road from Savanna IL to Minneapolis MN. Bald eagles soaring overhead, deer peeking out of the wooded hills and tugboats pushing barges up river.

Karen joined me in Regina SK and rode one week. We fought head winds across Sask., pedaling 14 hours one day to go 85 miles. The next day we covered the same distance in 6 hours with a tail wind.

Grandson Paul joined me in Edmonton AB. A few days later we biked into Dawson Creek, BC where the Alaskan Highway starts. Along the Alaskan Highway we encountered moose, deer, caribou, elk, buffalo, mountain sheep, wolves, black bear, grizzly bears, fox, lynx, coyotes, beaver, hares, porcupines, weasels, swans, eagles and owls.

At Whitehorse, Yukon Karla joined me and biked the final leg of the trip. In Fairbanks I switched to a mountain bike for the 200-miles of gravel road to the Arctic Circle. We spent the next night in Joy AK with the Carlsons who raised 23 children in a log cabin with no electricity, running water or indoor toilet.

On 24 June 1999 I biked across the Arctic Circle line, completing the 4,081-mile ride in 51 days. Worth the effort? You bet!   **$15.00**
ISBN 1-880675-03-X
[ ] AUSTRALIA FROM THE BACK OF A CAMEL

The 12 camels plodded through Rainbow Valley in the Australian outback. Kelsey, the author's 7-year-old granddaughter, nudged her 1,000-pound camel in the belly and Charcoal charged off in a cloud of dust, galloping to the head of the line. The author and 3 of his grandchildren were on a 7-day camel safari in the middle of the Australian desert. They spent 8 hours a day riding camels in search of caves with Aboriginal paintings, fossils, desert animals and unusual flora and fauna.

At night, the Johnsons slept on the ground around a huge fire to ward of the near-freezing temperature. It was winter in the desert, with daytime temperatures of 80 to 90F, but at night it dropped to 30 degrees F. They encountered wallabies, kangaroos, wedge-tailed eagles, dingos, emus and a variety of desert birds, lizards, snakes and spiders. The Johnsons sampled the desert foods, including eating a three-inch long witchery grub. The best part of the trip: "Running the camels across the dry lake-bed," Kelsey said. "Seeing how my grandchildren handled new situations," was Allen's reply. **$16.95**

ISBN 1-880675-02-1

[ ] BIKING ACROSS THE DEVIL'S BACKBONE

A 9-year-old and her grandfather pedaled 600 miles across the mid-West in search of adventure. Enroute they explored Cave-in-Rock on the Ohio River, the Garden of the Gods in southern Illinois, visited an ostrich farm in Mt. Vernon, spent the night with the monks at St. Meinrad Monastery, toured Lincoln's boyhood home in southern Indiana and pedaled over the razorback Devil's Backbone. Tracy maintained her good humor and high spirits while pedaling up to 65 miles a day through the hilly route in 95-degree heat. The best part of the trip? "The day at the monastery," replied Tracy. "Spending time with my granddaughter," explained Allen. **$15.95**

ISBN 1-880675-01-3

[ ] CANOEING THE WABASH

An adventure-packed 500-mile long trip canoeing down the Wabash River with the author and his 10-year-old grandson. From Fort Recovery, Ohio, they dragged the canoe through the shallow, upper Wabash, fought raging rapids and survived a 14-hour long thunder-lightening storm. At night the pair camped and fished along the banks of the river. They encountered deer, raccoons, muskrats, rabbits, beaver, gars and pileated woodpeckers during their 16-day journey along the still-wild river. The trip was a physical challenge and an educational experience. Along the river they visited Ft. Recovery, Tippecanoe Battlegrounds and the George Rogers Clark monument. After paddling one-quarter-million strokes they finally reached their destination—the Ohio River. The author weaves a tale of adventure, history and humor into a delightful package. **$13.95**

ISBN 1-880675-00-5

[ ]   DRIVE THROUGH RUSSIA? IMPOSSIBLE!

In 1981, the author and his wife rented a car and drove 4,000 miles through the Communist Soviet Union by themselves. This book describes the 3-week odyssey through the ancient countryside and modern bureaucracy. When the Johnsons first entered the Soviet Union, the officials informed them they would be staying the in the Pribaltiskaya Hotel that night in Leningrad. "What is the name of our hotel in Novgorod tomorrow night?" Allen asked. "It is not necessary for you to know. Tomorrow we will tell you where you will be staying." The author found that in the Soviet Union, information was power and the officials were very reluctant to give it away. With a basic understanding of the Russian language learned from 3 years of tutoring in Dayton before the trip, the Johnsons traveled from town to town, purchased food and gasoline, interpreted the meager road maps and visited with the Russian people. They found the people curious, kind and helpful. Travel with the Johnsons and enjoy a vivid picture of their daily discoveries, pleasures and frustrations.   **ISBN 0-553-06695-6**   **$10.95**

Order With This Convenient Coupon

Creative Enterprises
1040 Harvard Blvd.
Dayton OH 45406-5047

Please send me the books I have checked above. I am enclosing $_____ (please add $2.00 for postage/handling. Ohio residents add 7% tax). Send check or money order. You can also order from the Internet: **http://www.creative-enterprises.org, toll free from 888-BOOKS77, or E-mail allen45406@aol.com**

Name_____

Address_____

City_____ State _____ Zip Code _____

Allow 2—4 weeks for delivery.